This book is dedicated to the Divine Mother and my Sadguru Mata Amritanandamayi Devi (Amma).

"Ya Devi sarva bhuteshu Matru rupena samsthita
Namastasyai namasthasyai namastasyai namo namah"

I repeatedly bow to the Devi who exists as the mother in all beings.

HOW TO SURVIVE AND SUCCEED IN OFFICE AND HOME LIFE

WORK-LIFE BALANCE GUIDE FOR MID LEVEL EXECUTIVES

C. V. RAJAN

Contents

Contents

Contents

Foreword

When the author C. V. Rajan asked me to have a thorough look at his pre-press script of this book, I knew for sure that he was qualified to write such a book. I knew he was an Engineer who climbed up in the corporate ladder during his first 12 years of professional life, then quit it boldly (as he understood that he had no charm for a corporate life, despite being successful), then started his own 'Small Office Home Office' and ran it successfully for almost 2 decades, before opting to retire at an Ashram, seeking spiritual fulfillment of his life.

When I first glanced through the contents of this book, I could grasp that his own philosophies about work, life and the need of mixing spirituality in both are sprinkled generously across the book. One thing I doubted about the contents of the book was this -- it is not a book written exclusively for the title, but is more of a collection of several articles on both the prime subjects (Office matters and home matters). He confirmed that it was indeed so, as these articles were written by him on the Web across a couple of years in a couple of websites.

As I went through the first part of the book (Office matters) in depth, I could grasp the fact that the contents are indeed aimed at exccutives who start their career at the lower rungs of an organization and then grow up and mature as managers at the middle level. The chapters have been so judiciously lined up.

The contents have a different flavor unlike popular books on managerial excellence written by world-famous management gurus like Peter Drucker, John Adair, Dale Carnegie and the like. C. V. Rajan must have kept his eyes quite open to spot the lack of professionalism and mediocrity generally prevalent in many companies and their managers, and he seems to have written several of the chapters with a chuckle!

Except in a few chapters (like How to Conduct a Meeting) where he has given very specific pieces of advice (some of which are extremely valid and worthy), he has mostly given plenty of pointers to the readers to grasp what-is-what in a corporate life; he seems to have left the ways and means to tackle them to the readers' own ethos and strategies -- 'It is up to you to do what is appropriate for getting mental peace, success or survival' -- so to say.

Now, about the second half of the book -- on family life.

Right from those who are about to be married, those who are married and planning children, those who have to successfully tackle emotional issues with the spouse and also the financial headload to run the life, those who are lured by the maya of unbridled spending through Credit Cards, those who find it tough to keep the marital bond alive in the long run, and those who are at the verge of retirement -- this Second Half of the covers a plethora of matters related to family life.

As a reader, I was very impressed with certain specific chapters -- How to enjoy honeymoon bliss forever, Monogamy - Is it nature or nurture, Link between money and happiness, What is more important -- Your career or your family etc. I found lots of food for thought in them.

For sure, the author can easily be accused of possessing and preaching old-fashioned and archaic thinking that many people won't like to heed to!

But what to do? Certain spiritually sound principles, ethics, values, morals and advice that he has given without mincing words may taste bitter to many people, but if only they are ready to listen, life at home and office will be very smooth sailing indeed.

Deepika Arun
("Kadhai Osai")

Preface

What is the general goal of life for most people on the earth?

Get married and have a loving relationship with the spouse, have a nice family, rear children, have basic comforts in life well met, enjoy some luxuries, have a peaceful retired life and old age.

Hiccups do happen in married life in many predictable and unpredictable ways. Yet, people still really want to cling to family life and derive some joy out of it. Some get divorced and yet get remarried, because they want the love and intimacy with the spouse as a basic need in a family setup. Then there is the duty of taking care of the children.

Thus, everything revolves around family. The very purpose of working and earning money is predominantly to run the family. When the family life is smooth and cordial, when there is love and mutual care existing, then every strain of working in a job and earning money becomes truly meaningful.

Somewhere in this seemingly simple scheme of things, there is also an urge to have a 'successful career' as a potent psychological need in men. In the last couple of decades, such an urge has entered into the psyche of women too, thanks to the increased sense of gender equality across all developed and developing nations.

Successful career includes making quite good money, gaining posts, positions and promotions, climbing up the corporate ladder, and enjoying power, prestige and status.

Unfortunately, this urge attains such a monstrous proportion in some people's life that it can potentially damage the very basement -- a cordial family life!

That's where the need for the right work-life balance comes. Not everyone is destined to make it big in a corporate ladder. Not everyone is destined to be a superhuman role model.

There are a whole lot of people in the middle rungs of management who have their right to lead a 'successful life', where they can prove their worth and attain job satisfaction at office, and at the same time, have a very satisfactory family life.

This book is aimed to address that group and give some practical life lessons that can guide them to have a life which is well lived. This book is in two parts. The first part addresses office matters and the second half, the family matters.

Please note that this book is not a typical Self-help book aimed to generate the so-called billionaires, creators of new history, writers of overnight success stories and so on. It is for the mid-level, salaried executives who will be happy to find their 'successful middle path' and rightfully feel truly happy and proud of achieving it.

C. V. Rajan
Amritapuri (Jan 2023)

Acknowledgements

My heartfelt thanks to

- My readers who bought my first publication of this book in eBook format, and gave appreciative reviews and feedback. That gave me the confidence to bring the book in printed form.
- Deepika Arun, who has brought many of my Tamil stories alive in the form of Audio Books. Also for writing the foreword for this printed book.
- Hiral Varun for the beautiful digital art of my Sadguru Mata Amritanandamayi appearing at the end of this book.
- Srikala, Jayanti and Padmini for their constant support and encouragement to keep the writer in me alive.
- My wife Shanti for keeping the essence in me alive.

Part A

Survival and success guide

for the salaried executive

== At the office ==

CHAPTER ONE

The tell-tale signs of a typical Salaried Executive and an entrepreneur

Just a second: I was first thinking of putting this as the last chapter of this section, but later changed my mind. I felt it is better to understand the characteristics of a typical salaried executive, about whom the focus of this book is.

Since many salaried executives tend to nurture a dream of becoming an entrepreneur (or becoming a grand Startup) one day and it tempts them to be the worthiest ideal, let us understand the different mindsets of these two categories.

Can all those who work as employees become entrepreneurs one day? Not all! Some are simply born and destined to work under somebody else; their nature and characteristics are different from those of an entrepreneur.

Let us understand this clearly. Not everyone is equipped to become an entrepreneur. If this is understood clearly, many start-up failures could be avoided!

Some of the typical "employee" characteristics are listed below:

1. Desire for steady income

They will be very particular about getting a secure, predictable and steady weekly/ monthly income. They would like to have the best control over their income and expenditure, their capacity to borrow and repay.

2. Lack of initiative

Some of them, particularly in the lower rungs of the corporate ladder, will be comfortable and content in doing the work assigned to them; they will not be too enthusiastic in taking self-propelled initiatives; When it comes to making decisions, they would find it rather convenient to leave them to the boss.

3. No risk

They would not like to take any huge risk at their own cost; They may be excellent managers who have the capacity to make the right decisions and take calculated risks within their scope of responsibility in the organization they work for. But, they make sure that they have the relevant safeguards in place; the safeguards are in the form of higher managerial support and the company's capacity to absorb the consequences, if their risk-taking backfires.

4. Designation consciousness

They take pride in their designations, their ascent in the corporate ladder, the perks and privileges associated with their position in the organization, and the security and prestige the job gives to their social and family life. Those who have grown to very respectable positions in their organizations know pretty well that some of the perks they enjoy could not be dreamed of by many entrepreneurs who do business with their organization.

5. "Freedom - a myth"

In their opinion, the pet idea of a typical entrepreneur, the idea of being a master of their own affairs and not being answerable to any big boss above is not true in a real sense. In an organization, you have to be answerable to your boss. In the case of an entrepreneur, he has to be answerable to his customer, to the investors, to their bankers etc. The customer is ultimately the big boss. So, their line of argument is: if independence is the motivating factor, it is non-existent even if you are self-employed.

6. No mastery

Some of them will be jacks of all trades, but masters of none; They would not have acquired any focused mastery in any line of activity that they can confidently and independently handle. When it comes to specifics to nuts and bolts, they will be at a loss to handle the spanner!

It could be seen that for people of aforesaid nature, working for salary is the best option and they are quite right in their choice. However successful they might be in their managerial spirit and administrative capabilities, they may not blossom to become entrepreneurs.

Entrepreneurial spirit

On the other side of the fence, those who have the entrepreneurial spirit in them have the following characteristics:

1. A dreamer & a risk-taker

They have a dream to realize; a pet idea that they believe will work; They are willing to pump in every breath of theirs to bring life to their dream. They do not mind taking huge risks if their inner voice keeps saying "you can do it". They know pretty well that no worthwhile success could be achieved without taking a calculated risk.

2. *Not status-conscious*

They are least concerned about the post, position, status, respectability, etc in the early stages of working to realize their dreams, and they are confident that once they succeed, everything else will fall in place. Being the chief of their own little province is more adorable to them than being one of the ministers of a huge empire.

3. *Not too worried about steady income*

They are flexible enough to be prepared to live with unsteady and unpredictable income. Either they guard themselves against ups and downs by judicious savings or by jumping into the river and trying to swim against all odds.

4. *Being their own masters*

They take pride in calling their own shots. It is not that they do not know the customer is the ultimate boss. They know they are answerable to their customers and other stakeholders. But the difference, in their perception, is that they have the freedom to choose which customer to serve or not to serve. By virtue of their risk-taking capacity, they can exercise this freedom at will and be bold enough to face the consequences, unlike their counterparts at the corporate ladder.

5. *"I know my job"*

They have their niche areas where they are quite confident about their knowledge and expertise; When a situation demands, the entrepreneur has no qualms to do the role of a mechanic and be ready to do a blue-collared job at will without bothering about prestige.

Yes. Entrepreneurs are made of different and sterner stuff. Just because a person of a deeply-etched 'employee' mindset has found some reasons to be disgruntled with his current way of life, he cannot simply jump into the self-employment bandwagon and repeat his past success as an employee.

Just because one had been denied a rightful promotion or had been sidelined in the organization despite proven technical merits; just because one had faced frustrations because of a stupid boss, or a suicidal corporate decision despite one's warnings; just because one did not like the new post or transfer -- a person of a salaried class should not think of becoming an entrepreneur and make a success of it.

The salaried executive need not think that his status is somewhat less-than-ideal in comparison with an entrepreneur. The world goes on smoothly with a proper balance between employers and employees. Both are important and have their place in the running of the universal business of God.

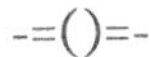

CHAPTER TWO

Ways to Be a Success on the Job - Strategies for getting yourself Promoted

Success on the job has several scales to measure. One is your pay rise, another is your growth in the organizational ladder and the third is your popularity/ respectability/ indispensability in the organization. Promotion and rise in the corporate ladder are essential for everyone who wants to feel proud of his worth.

Promotions do not easily come on their own. You have to develop skills, merits and strategies to get yourself promoted ahead of competing colleagues.

To be successful, you have to have certain capabilities. They include:

- Your working skills, technical (job-related) knowledge, producing results as per expectations by your boss or as per targets given to you, and better still, exceeding them.
- Administrative skills - in managing people, tasks, plans, and schedules. This also includes good communication skills.
- Interpersonal skills - moving well with colleagues, subordinates, and seniors and also the knack of skillfully handling office

politics and power games.

Being capable in any one of the above three broad categories may help you to get elevated to a certain level only in the organization; for consistency in tasting success, you must be proficient in ALL these categories.

Technical skill matters - only to an extent

Many of us, in judging competence in ourselves to become successful, mostly restrict ourselves to the first point. Of course, it is one of the MAJOR criteria in judging an employee. Many times, at lower rungs of the organizational ladder, working skill is a major quality that rightfully gets its due share of prominence in fetching a pay rise or a promotion.

However, truly technically competent people generally have a problem. They are mostly too egoistic. Even if they are not, recognition of their expertise (by themselves or by others in comparison with colleagues and even bosses) makes them egoistic over a period of time! Highly skilled, knowledgeable and competent people develop a tendency to 'look down' at incompetent people - and many times it includes the boss! Intentionally or unintentionally, this 'looking down' gets expressed in reactions, gestures, and at times, even in words. This will prove to be counterproductive sooner or later.

Being a 'specialist' has its advantages only up to certain levels in the organizational ladder. Growing up in an organization beyond a level involves taking up more responsibilities, covering more of hither-to-unfamiliar turf, managing more people, and getting things done from those who themselves are 'specialists'. Thus a natural evolution from a 'specialist' to a 'generalist' will pave success on the job in the long run.

Be enthusiastic and willing to take up responsibility

While hard work is a respected quality, a person who works hard but is unwilling to take responsibility for the quality/ outcome of his efforts and expects his boss to take the blame if something goes wrong, is not the one who is fit to grow in the organization.

Demonstrate decisiveness

You should not be the type who runs up to your boss every time to take instructions, even where you yourself should have used your sense of judgment. This attitude may please many bosses, as it gives them a false sense of pride. But an indecisive person is not fit for successful growth in the organization in the long run.

When you encounter a problem, are you behaving as a part of the problem or part of a solution? Where a solution is within your knowledge but beyond your powers of execution, are you approaching your boss with the problem along with a well-thought-out solution? If yes, you are poised for tasting success on the job.

Stretch a bit more

If you are a service engineer, do you willingly put extra working hours at the customer's site to make the critical machine run at the crucial juncture without expecting any special consideration for it? If you are an Accounts clerk, do you willingly extend a helping hand to the Sales Executive to sort out a dispute with a customer regarding a tax issue without saying 'it is not my work?' Then you are a potential candidate to taste success in the organization.

Observe and learn - be prepared to step in
Make yourself fit to shoulder the next higher position by observing and learning from what your boss is doing.

- What sort of correspondence does he do?
- What sort of reports does he make?
- What sort of decisions does he take?
- What sort of additional work is he doing?

- What sort of meetings does he attend and does he conduct?
- What sort of additional skill-sets does he possess at his level?
- What sort of mistakes is he committing?
- What are the areas he is supposed to be thorough but is really not?
- What sort of weaknesses does he display and how should a better boss avoid them?

Keep asking these questions; observe and learn. Keep reading books on managerial effectiveness, good managerial methods, and practices written by successful businessmen and management gurus.

Never shy away from actively participating or from presenting your ideas and views in meetings attended by higher echelons in management. BE AND BECOME VISIBLE. Get noticed.

Improve your communication skills

It is one of the most important aspects for one to deserve a promotion. Both verbal and written communication skills play a very significant role in your career. Some people are good at verbal communication but too poor or lazy in putting things in writing. Use of correct language, grammar, clarity, and crispness in your emails and letters, reports and presentations, your promptness in responding to mails, etc are very essential in written communications.

Know one thing for sure. A majority of people are poor in written communications. If you can demonstrate your skills in it, you are better qualified for promotion.

Improve your qualifications

There are organizations that lay stress on certain minimum educational qualifications for consideration to certain higher managerial positions. By joining part-time courses and improving your qualifications will help you to grow to higher positions. By not missing to attend any in-house training programs and by demonstrating your competence in such programs, you can look for promotional opportunities.

Diversify

Grabbing an opportunity to horizontally move in an organization (for example, a Maintenance Manager, opting to take up the role of a Production Manager which in reality may not be a promotion) will help you get acquainted with newer skills and pave way for future promotions on a faster lane.

Be loyal to your organization

This trait is gradually diminishing in the present-day culture of too frequent job-hopping. However, if you demonstrate your identification with the goals and values of the organization, if you do not act as a parasite to stealthily enjoy the perks and privileges from the organization by some devious means, then you stand a far better chance in growing quickly in the organization.

A person with a long-standing experience of working in the organization has the core values of the organization better imbibed in him than someone who joined relatively recently. Successful companies always maintain a fair ratio of old blood and fresh blood in the veins of the organization. Loyalty pays.

Respect the boss

A boss is a boss whether he is in that position deservingly or undeservedly. He has his ego to be buttressed, whether he is competent or not. If he develops a grouse against you, he won't mind ignoring you in preference to a less competent but more amenable colleague of yours.

Even if the boss is incompetent, he is bound to be there till the time his vulnerability gets exposed. Whether you like it or not, give him due respect to his position and do not rub him at the wrong side. At the same time, improve your capabilities to fit into his shoes if and when the opportune moment arrives.

Beyond a level, it is interpersonal skills that matter

You may get promoted to a couple of higher levels by the strength of your work/ technical competence; but if you do not hone your competence in interpersonal skills, your weakness in this area starts getting exposed. You may get a reputation as a task-master, but lose cordial relationships with colleagues and subordinates.

In meetings with higher-ups, your body language, verbal skills, use of phrases, assertiveness, politeness combined with firmness, your appreciation or criticism about policy matters - everything will be keenly watched and judged.

As one moves up in the higher echelons of management, competence in man-management takes priority over core skills. As already seen earlier, many technically competent people get a beating in this area and they fail to grasp the change of perception needed at higher levels. One must have the capacity to manage the good, bad, and the ugly - not only among those under his stewardship but also among those who are up above in the pecking order.

In other words, for your growth and success, your EQ (Emotional Quotient) takes precedence over your IQ (Intelligent Quotient).

Improve your visibility

By your active and energetic participation in corporate meetings, sales conferences, product promotional campaigns, etc., make yourself visible to the higher echelons of management. Sometimes, many bosses have the tendency to 'hide' their smart subordinates in order to take all the credits for themselves. This sort of exposure to a higher managerial level will be quite helpful in countering your boss's maneuvers in thwarting your growth in the organization.

Over and above good interpersonal skills, if you have the guts and inclination, you can develop political skills like maneuvering, manipulation, and personality-oriented loyalty to the centers of power in the organization. This is one channel for quicker success, which of course has its own risks!

Alternatively, you should develop excellent diplomatic skills to stay clean and clear of any murky politics and groups inside the organization. Power centers may keep changing from time to time. Being identified with one 'group' may work out advantageous at one time and it may backfire at some other time. Non-identification with any group may always be a safer strategy for promotions in the long run.

Become invaluable

Higher management should know your 'true value' to the organization, which is possible only when your contribution to the organization is far ahead of the pay and perks you receive. If you are perceived to be a coveted candidate available for a grab by competitors, your value increases multifold. This way, a job offer from a competitor or from another prestigious organization can become a powerful tool for negotiating and getting a promotion within your organization. But remember that this is a potential tool that has the power to backfire too!

As long as you develop yourself as a multi-faceted personality who is competent in all the aspects discussed, success is assured in your career.

-=()=-

CHAPTER THREE

How to Establish Trust between you and your Boss

Trustworthiness is a character trait that will keep you in good stead in life and your gaining the trust of your boss is no exception. If you and your boss are new to each other, of course, it takes some time to make the correct judgment about each other's behavior, character, and trustworthiness. But the sooner you are able to establish trustworthiness with your boss, the better for you in your career progression.

Here are some tips for you to establish trust between you and your boss:

Report back voluntarily even when the boss forgets

The boss might assign a specific task to you and he may forget to follow up with you on it due to his busy engagements. Do not take his silence for granted to postpone the task with the idea that as and when he asks about it, you can take it up. Carry out his instructions and report to him voluntarily on the outcome and he will definitely get a feeling that you can be relied upon to carry out tasks without chasing up.

Take notes

When your boss calls you for a one-to-one meeting and issues several instructions to carry out, scribble them in your notepad right in front of him, point by point. This will not only help you to carry out the tasks systematically later but will also impress your boss that you are a person quite serious in taking action with a written agenda and that you do not intend to give any excuse later saying "I forgot" or worse still, saying "I am afraid you didn't instruct me so during the last meeting".

Be thorough in your paper/ written work

Many people shun paperwork or written work considering it to be bureaucratic and time-consuming. The boss may want you to prepare minutes of a meeting or send emails to higher-ups on specific matters discussed. A subordinate who volunteers to do such paperwork and also does it thoroughly is immediately recognized as trustworthy.

Be honest on money matters

The trustworthiness of a person is best judged in the matters of handling money and finance. When you collect advance from the office for some expenses, are you prompt in settling the accounts by submitting the necessary bills and documents subsequently? Are your transactions with suppliers and subcontractors open and transparent? Do you restrict your spending within your budget and do you clearly demonstrate your adherence to spending norms and limits commensurate with your position in the organization? As long as your boss observes that you are honest and transparent in these matters, his trust in you will increase multifold.

The trustworthiness of a boss too will be keenly observed by subordinates. Does the boss display 'cleanliness' in matters of money? Are his transactions transparent in cash-rich contracts?

Can his verbal statements, instructions, commitments, and promises be taken as good as written ones? Does he demonstrate fair play without favoritism in recognizing and rewarding merit?

The trust between the boss and subordinate must always be two-way for a healthy relationship between them for the betterment of the organization.

-=()=-

CHAPTER FOUR

How to Deal with the Boss who is Disruptive

Dealing with a boss who is disruptive requires lots of tact, patience, level headedness, and street-smartness. A boss is a boss whether you like it or not, whether he is cooperative or disruptive. Rubbing at the wrong side of the boss should be avoided at all costs but coaxing, manipulating, diverting, and subverting a boss are all acceptable practices as long as you are smart enough!

A disruptive boss may act in several ways and you should have appropriate tactics to ward off his trouble. Here are some cases and some suggestions:

Disrupting your work by conducting unwanted meetings

Many bosses have so much idle time that in order to keep themselves engaged, they conduct meetings! Many bosses would like to call all and sundry to the meetings and review matters with each one of them, while others in the meeting may have nothing to contribute.

One tactic you can try is to ask a subordinate beforehand to give a call to you after a predetermined time when your role in the meeting would normally be over. It could be in the guise of a customer waiting to meet you; it could be about some urgent information that the head office seeks from you 'immediately'.

Pretend that it is an emergency and request your boss to excuse you and permit you to leave the meeting!

Disrupting your work by calling for a one-to-one discussion

If you are quite sure that the call is not meant to be on any serious issue but just a ploy for the boss to idle away his time, tell him that you will come and meet him in the next half an hour (or at a time just before lunch). Don't give him any reason until he insists. Your voice should express a feeling as though you are very busy on a very important task; it should deter him from asking the reason!

Your boss comes to your seat and wastes your time

This is an extremely difficult situation. Some tactics to get rid of the boss under the situation require good acting skills. You can seek his excuse to visit the toilet as you have some uneasy rumbling in your stomach. You can call your subordinate to your seat, start discussing some problems or issues and drag the time. Your boss may get bored and leave the seat. You can pretend as though you have given an appointment to somebody at his office and seek an excuse to leave the place. Go to the canteen, and return after a while. There is a danger in this tactic. Your idle boss too may be visiting the canteen to kill his time, once you dispose of him!

Your boss frequently changes your work in hand and wants you to do something else

Do what he says and put the blame on your boss at the appropriate time and at the appropriate place when things go awry. "I did only as per your instructions" should be your refrain.

We can go on and on discussing various tactics this way. But the important point to be noted is that you should be confident and manipulative enough to do things in your own way, keeping the tasks and priorities as demanded by your work. But you should make your boss feel as though whatever you are doing or not doing is exactly as per his directions!

-=()=-

CHAPTER FIVE

How to handle conflicts with the boss - Useful and Practical Hints

Unless you are an abominable yes-man, some conflicts of opinions, disagreement about decisions made, subtle and not-so-subtle ego clashes, etc can happen between you and your boss. When you don't agree with your boss, the way to tackle the problem can range from a simple to a dangerously complex way, depending on the complexity of the issue and the personality traits you and your boss have.

There can be so many permutations of personality traits between the boss and the subordinate that can dictate the way the disagreement with the boss is tackled. The boss can be assertive, egoistic, level-headed, or meek. The subordinate too can be classified likewise. When there is a disagreement between the boss and the subordinate, there can be 16 ways the equation between them that can play in handling the dispute.

Before giving any generic advice on what to do when you don't agree with the boss, let us just see a few sample combinations to understand how different ways of tackling the conflict can arise in case of a disagreement.

Assertive Boss versus Meek Subordinate

The outcome is obvious. The boss dictates and the subordinate agrees, gulping his disagreement down his throat. If the subordinate is proved to be right at the end, he chuckles secretly and boasts about his foresight to his wife!

Meek Boss versus Assertive Subordinate

The subordinate knows well that he can manipulate his boss to bring him to his line of thinking and he can talk his way through to convince the boss; When things go awry, the boss, being the boss, will say, "I told you so, but you were adamant. I always believe in giving a free hand to my subordinates so that they learn from mistakes"!

Egoistic Boss Versus Egoistic Subordinate

A minor clash of the titans will result. For both of them, prestige is more important than the facts behind the dispute. When the subordinate takes the bull by the horns, he knows pretty well that if the outcome of the disputed decision does not work in his favor, he may not be in a position to continue in his job for long. Either he has to continue to fight or take a flight.

Egoistic Boss Versus Level Headed Subordinate

What is life if full of care there's no conflict with the boss to face?

The subordinate knows pretty well that he is more right than his boss but also knows that he cannot convince his boss that easily. Being level-headed, he can take several recourses to handle the disagreement with the boss. Some of them are given below:

When the boss vehemently opposes the subordinate's counterpoints, the subordinate buys time; He suggests that the matter can be reviewed afresh after a couple of days. This way, there is a fair chance that the ego of the boss cools down and he can see things more objectively in the next review.

The subordinate clearly expresses his disagreements politely to his boss at the same time adding a statement like this: "but if you still wish to proceed as it is, I will put forth my full cooperation to you, despite all my objections. You can rest assured about it." This statement is most likely to buttress the ego of the boss. He may even show the willingness to review the matter now.

Level headed boss versus level headed subordinate

Most unlikely combo! But if it exists, it is the best for the organization. The subordinate freely and fearlessly discusses what he disagrees with the boss and the boss listens. They exchange ideas, argue with each other, and in the end, common sense prevails.

Thus, obviously, the one-to-one equation between the boss and the subordinate can offer so much variety in tackling the conflicts between the boss and the subordinate. We have seen only a few combos in the above analysis and as we saw at the beginning, there is scope for so much more combos in the duo.

Now coming to generic advice to tackle disagreement with the boss.

If you are smart and analytical enough, your strategy should be based on what sort of combo exists between you and the boss in the above examples.

Irrespective of whether the boss has an upper hand or you have, the most sensible advice is: never rub at the ego of the boss. Whether smart, meek, idiotic, or level-headed, every person has his ego and would always like it to be buttressed. Even a cold-blooded murderer has a justification for what he did and mostly remains unapologetic at that. Diplomacy is the watchword in dealing with the boss; watch your words. Never utter the following, even if you are 100% justified: "I am more experienced on these matters than you", "I am sorry to say, you are absolutely wrong". "My boss in my erstwhile company did the same mistake and he had to regret it for life"

Though it is very difficult, try to segregate the issue from the personality. After a heated argument and disagreement in opinions, can you exchange a very pleasant "Good morning" with him the next day and cut a joke with him across a cup of coffee at the cafeteria?

Avoid back-biting. This is another extremely difficult instinct to curtail. Criticizing and joking about the boss with colleagues in hushed tones during lunchtime is the pastime for most of us. Beware. There will always be black sheep in the crowd.

Put it in writing. If you are 100% sure that your boss' decision or action is detrimental to the overall interest of the company, put it into the record by writing in some way - a gist of discussions, or minutes of the meeting, or simple handwritten notes in the files, or an internal memo, whatever - with the right dose of diplomacy for the boss' review, with a copy marked to his higher-ups, if feasible. This way, you make your genuine objections known to the higher powers to whom the boss is answerable. Though the boss may detest such a move, he cannot but take a fresh review to answer likely questions from his higher-ups.

Even if the boss bulldozes your objections, your viewpoints are there in the file to save your skin in case of a catastrophe. Who knows, this action may even facilitate your elevation to replace your boss!

Never underestimate the clout of a 'the seemingly weak' boss. If you have a communication channel to subvert your boss and take recourse to higher-ups, your boss too may have his own, through which he can do damage to your career, by distorting the facts. So, unless you are 100% sure and justified, do not try to subvert your boss.

To sum up, in a disagreement with the boss, the one and final test of fire is your honest answer to this question: "Is my objection based on what is good for the organization and not what is good for my selfish motives and egotistic cravings?"

CHAPTER SIX

How to Handle the Boss who Plays Favorites

Bosses are neither robots nor computers who simply work according to the program, commands and logic. They are human beings with their share of limitations in the head and heart. In any given situation, most people, including the bosses, act based on emotions and justify their actions by logic.

Playing favoritism by bosses is part of the occupational hazard for any employee. At one end, meek bosses lacking competence, managerial prowess and self-confidence are those who predominantly play favoritism. At another end, very powerful bosses who are happy to have 'yes men' around them too play favorites.

The type of personality that a subordinate possesses generally determines the way to handle a boss who plays favorites.

Meek but amenable subordinates

The best strategy for such subordinates is to play by the tunes of the boss so as to enter into his good books and become one of his favorites. Meek subordinates who lack competence generally have much less egotism and in fact, dancing to the tunes of the boss rather than showing work competence is the naturally best choice for their career growth.

Over-smart subordinates

Over-smart subordinates have the competence to play politics better than the boss. They know the knack of locating the power center amidst the next two or three layers of managers. If the immediate boss happens to be the power center, they will go all out to woo the boss, after keenly analyzing his needs, wants, expectations and weaknesses. If the power center is elsewhere, they would not mind doing everything to reach closer to that center, and in the process, they will take the calculated risk of ignoring or circumventing their own boss.

Competent but egoistic subordinates

Such subordinates are normally those who frequently lose the goodwill of their bosses because they display an 'I know better than you' attitude. Their approach will normally be confrontational. Their ego will not permit them to bend to the extraneous expectations of the bosses and they will normally expect rewards as a matter of right to their efficiency and performance. It is always better either for the boss or for the subordinate to get him relieved from the team and transferred to another team or department so that the bickering is minimized. Some people would opt to move out of the company – for them, taking flight is better than a fight.

Level headed and mature subordinates

They will act according to the merit and temperament of the boss. If they know for sure that the boss has obvious limitations in managerial capacity, they will bide their time for the boss to get exposed; while they will not act with a confrontationist attitude, they will, however, make sure to display their competence and smartness to a couple of levels above the boss (e.g. through confident talking, by offering insightful and competent suggestions in meetings attended by higher-ups) and make others understand that they are indeed meritorious for taking up higher responsibilities in future.

Whatever be the strategy, it is always best to avoid a direct confrontational attitude; a person who is able to move well with people above, below, and at his peer level is normally considered good managerial material from the point of view of personnel management.

CHAPTER SEVEN

What to do when competence is ignored and Slacker one Receives Favor from the Boss

This is one common grouse most employees tend to nurture -- 'I am OK but the boss is NOT OK' syndrome! No employee ever writes in his self-appraisal that he has not performed to the expected standards. But the bosses have different scales of measurement and those yardsticks need not be without their errors of measurement too. It is part and parcel of an organized office setup.

In deciding the competence of a subordinate (from the point of giving an annual increment or a promotion or a prestigious recognition) the reviews will not take place just based on the recommendations of the immediate boss alone.

At higher levels of management, rewarding an employee may have several strings attached, other than the wishes and judgment of the immediate boss, however honest and accurate it may be.

Here is one real-life example.

A technical sales executive in a machine tool firm was working hard for the past year to do all the pre-sales technical spadework to grab a huge order from a prestigious customer. The machines were to be imported from abroad in the form of subassemblies. They had to be assembled, wired, and tooled-up in their factory before it was delivered. The Technical Sales Executive had undertaken the responsibility of tooling up the machines and conducting trials of the customers' sample components at the user's site after delivery.

There was a time gap of 5 months in between the booking of orders and final delivery. The executive was relatively free during this period, and he was handling some other minor responsibilities at that period. It was then the annual appraisal took place. The executive's boss knew pretty well how much hard work he had put in and what an amount of responsibility he still held till the machines were approved at the customer's site. The fact was that no other executive under him was technically competent to shoulder that huge responsibility. He naturally gave the highest rating and recommended a double-increment for his subordinate.

Unfortunately for the Executive, it was the period when the incumbent General Manager of the branch (who also knew the capabilities and importance of the executive) got transferred and a new GM took over.

As the new GM had one-to-one conversations with the executives of the branch as a prelude to taking final decisions on their increments, he asked this executive, "So, what are you doing right now?"

The poor executive, with all honesty, mentioned his past and upcoming responsibilities, adding that he was presently relatively free, doing minor tasks.

That, unfortunately, ended him up with just getting a normal increment, while, another peer-level executive, in another department in his office, who was extremely busy doing mundane tasks and doing them well, got away with a double increment!

Naturally, the executive was unhappy. His immediate boss, who too felt bad that his recommendation was ignored, raised the matter with the GM. The reply he got was, "That fellow is not having enough work in the current 4-5 months, no? Who will pay a double increment for him?"

While the above example demonstrates the subjective nature of assessing competence, there are indeed real, objective aspects of competence, expected from the subordinates from the higher management point of view.

We have already seen them in some of the earlier chapters. At the risk of repetition, let me make a revisit of those aspects again, in the current context.

When we say competence, the counter-question is, Competence in what?

In a workplace, you need competence in

- Your working skills, technical (job-related) knowledge, producing results as per expectations by your boss or as per targets given to you and if possible, exceeding them.
- In moving well with colleagues, subordinates, and seniors i.e. interpersonal skills
- Administration in managing people, tasks, plans, schedules and also office politics and power games.

Many of us, in judging competence in ourselves, mostly restrict ourselves to the first point. Of course, it is one of the major criteria in judging an employee, and only by the strength of it, every organization is able to produce results. Many a time, at lower rungs of the organizational ladder, working skills is a major quality that should rightly get its due share of prominence in grabbing a boss' attention.

However, truly competent people generally have a problem. They are too egoistic. Even if they are not, recognition of their competence (by themselves or by others in comparison with colleagues and even bosses) makes them egoistic over a period of time! Highly skilled, knowledgeable and competent people develop a tendency to 'look down' at incompetent people, and many times it may include the boss too! Intentionally or unintentionally, this 'looking down' gets expressed in reactions, gestures and at times, even in words.

Even the boss is only a human being and he has his ego to be buttressed, whether he is competent or otherwise. If he develops a grouse against you, he won't mind ignoring you in preference to a less competent but more amenable person. A boss is a boss whether he deserves to be in that position or not. Your judgment about him (even if it is hundred percent accurate) does not really matter; his position has been given to him by his higher-ups and it is what matters.

So, lesson number one to learn is: if you are not in the favor of your boss, then, even if you can not do anything artificially to keep him in good humor, at least be careful in giving him due respect to his position and do not rub him on the wrong side.

This is where point number (2) Interpersonal skills gains importance. You may get promoted to a couple of higher levels by the strength of your work competence; but if you do not hone your competence in interpersonal skills, your weakness in this area starts getting exposed. You may get a reputation as a task-master, but lose cordial relationships with colleagues and subordinates.

In meetings with higher-ups, your body language, use of phrases, your criticism about policy matters, etc may acquire a sharper tinge and this may not be to the liking of many. You may figure in unofficial chit-chats like this: "What he talks makes sense, but he seems to think all others are idiots". In other words, your competence gets noticed but your egotism gets you depreciated.

As one moves up in the higher echelons of management, competence in man-management takes priority over core skills. Many technically competent people get a beating in this area and they fail to grasp the change of perception needed at these levels. One must have the capacity to manage the good, bad, and ugly not only among those under his stewardship but also among those who are up above in the pecking order. Over and above good interpersonal skills, you have to develop political skills like maneuvering, manipulation, personality-oriented loyalty to the organization, etc.

Thus, if you keep harping on your competence in your core skills alone, it is quite natural that you will be ignored over a period of time. But becoming manipulative, engaging in dirty office politics, etc may not be palatable to many straightforward players. It is not that all organizations are infested with such complications. If you feel that your organization is not suited to your principles and values, or your style of management, it is high time you look for alternative avenues.

But the happenings in an organization need not be well definable as we have discussed above. There could be lot of aberrations like:

- an incompetent boss, preferring less competent sub-ordinates (so that his sense of comfort is not disturbed)
- a competent boss preferring incompetent subordinates (so that his 'towering' position is not disturbed, nor threatened)
- a competent boss falling prey to 'excessive display of respect and reverence' by an incompetent person and favoring him in return.
- a boss having prejudices against a race, religion or sect, etc.

It is always easy to build a superlative self-image about ourselves without a balanced self-analysis and complain about our boss. It is also possible that the bosses have inherent weaknesses to ignore a competent person. Our reactions to such situations thus range from emotional to logical. The corrective course of action too depends on our emotions or logic or a mixture of both.

CHAPTER EIGHT

Helping a coworker who did not get his promotion

The emotional status of the coworker is going to be in one way if he lost the promotion amidst other competing colleagues excluding you; it will be altogether different if he lost the promotion by competing against you and you were the one to get the coveted post. So, the ways of helping the coworker to come out of his bruised feelings will have to be different.

If the co-worker did not get a promotion and you were unconnected with that, it is far easier to offer helpful counsel to bring him back to normalcy. The process will be facilitated further if you happen to be a good friend of his, whereby he can freely confide his emotions to you and also be willing to take your counsel.

If the colleague was truly meritorious and deserving to get the promotion, but failed on account of other reasons, you can always highlight his positive strengths and reassure him that merit will never go unnoticed and it will not go unrewarded. You can convince him saying perhaps the time is not ripe for him to get his due reward or perhaps he is destined to get something bigger and better.

As a way of consoling him, you can also point out the pitfalls associated with any promotion – like added burden of responsibilities, possibility of getting transferred to an undesirable locations, working and dealing with too demanding and unreasonable bosses, the difficulty of managing more man-power, possible loss of mental peace and the possible demand of more time to be spent at the office, etc. Anyone looking for a promotion would not have probably thought seriously of all these matters. At a time when not getting the promotion looks to be a great loss, these "alternative points of view" can really help one to think from a different angle and feel relieved for a while.

If the person who did not get the promotion lost on account of competing with a better qualified and truly meritorious person, then the counseling has to be done in a different way. Indirectly, but not hurting the lost co-worker's ego, this reality may be conveyed in subtle ways. Words like "You see, sometimes it is not just hard work but it is smart work that gets rewarded; you should know how to work smarter than before, and the bosses should also come to know that you are smart enough to hold higher responsibilities; just observe how successful people work and learn from them".

If the coworker lost the promotion in competition with you, the last thing you should project is that you are more meritorious and deserving than him. If you want your relationship to continue well and if the person is going to be your subordinate hereafter, then you should be smart enough to win his heart, not by bossing around, but by continuing to treat him as a colleague and a worthy teammate.

Accompanying him to the canteen, meeting him casually at weekends, or going to movies together (if you had been doing it earlier) may have to be continued. Sometimes, complaining to him about the stresses and pains associated with the new responsibilities may even help him to feel relieved that he didn't entangle himself into them, fortunately. By your talk, body gestures, or official interactions, you should try to maintain a posture wherein your co-worker will not feel that he is belittled just because he lost in competition with you.

Good interpersonal skills are needed in handling such emotional issues. Those who are gifted with those skills will evolve to become good man-managers in the future.

-=()=-

CHAPTER NINE

Ways Part-time Jobs can help you Gain Experience

When you work in a part-time job, it means your prime time is deployed in something else, either a full-time job, at studies, or at home-making. A Part-time job does not only fetch you the extra cash you need but also brings along with it a valuable experience that can enhance your worth.

A part-time job may not be to do with your core skills and experience, but if it does, it is an added advantage for you. If it doesn't, it is all the more beneficial for you to gain experience, because, if the part-time job were not to be there, you may not perhaps get exposed to those experiences.

Let us assume, for example, that your full-time job confines you to technical work without the need for interpersonal dealings, but your part-time job is to do with lots of interaction with people, (say, a sales job). Remember that for any staff to grow to become a manager one day, the top-most skill needed is to manage people. In a part-time sales job, you will get exposed to dealing with a variety of people with varying temperaments, moods, and tastes.

A sales job develops patience, a pleasant demeanor in interpersonal dealings and a capacity to convince people through your talking skills. Thus, without effort, you are acquiring skills that will be valuable to you for your future growth, through this part-time job.

No job is exclusively earmarked for dull heads. Every job has its nuance and there are always knacks of doing things better, faster, and smarter in any job. In a part-time job, you will get exposed to opportunities to develop those knacks and skills, if only you are smart enough to learn them. These skills may not have anything to do with your full-time job today, but no skill developed inside you goes to waste. At the right time at the most opportune moment, the skill acquired by you in your part-time job will come in handy and be a blessing.

Employers always love to recruit people who are willing to work hard and long. Working in a part-time job means you have the quality of hard work and you are not the type who whiles away your free time in some unproductive way. This could be a quality that impresses a future employer who may be willing to offer a good salary to employ you, leading to a situation where working part-time to earn extra money may become a thing of the past.

CHAPTER TEN

Customer service is not for everybody

To become a success in any job, one requires technical skills, interpersonal skills and a mental aptitude as well as an attitude that fits well with the nature of the job. If you ask what qualities are needed for customer service, it is your technical expertise in solving problems, in maintaining your cool even when tempers are rising at the customer end, a willingness to please the customers in all adverse circumstances, and be happy in doing it.

Customer service requires the right attitude. Highly egoistic people who have a high degree of "self-rightist" attitude, who are short-tempered, who have less patience, who are too argumentative, who do not have the restraint of their tongue from speaking at the wrong time, and who have bureaucratic tendencies are not the fit persons to work at customer service.

From the point of view of workload, if you are a service engineer who has to go and repair malfunctioning products supplied by your firm at the customer's works, then you have to be prepared to spend long working hours without looking at the clock to solve the problem in a critical machinery. The customer may expect you to be an expert and a jack of all trades to solve the problem at the drop of the hat; the customer may continually breathe behind your neck and put pressure on you to solve the problem without allowing adequate time for you to go into the root cause of the problem.

At times, your company may expect you to travel to far-off places without giving adequate time for you to plan your travel or without giving any consideration to any of your personal or family problems.

In practical reality, not all rightly qualified persons would want to work in customer service. A mechanical engineer may be quite good at solving technical problems as part of customer service, but he may not be endowed with many other qualities that are needed in addition to technical virtuosity, like patience, politeness and controlling rising of temper when offended.

While some can tackle customers with common sense, it may be extremely difficult for them to tackle illogical and irrational customers who try acting too smart. Some professionals, if they are confident that they are 100% right, can become quite argumentative with customers and they may not concede to any illogical demands, for the sake of satisfying the customer.

There are some people who become very rigid if they are repeatedly pressed to do something that they are not convinced of. A right customer-oriented approach would require flexibility and non-rigidity. Those who are too principled or bureaucratic cannot do a satisfactory job at customer service.

Customer service is not for everybody. No wonder some people would not end up there, even if they are technically qualified for the job.

-=()=-

CHAPTER ELEVEN

The transition – from being a subordinate to a manager – How being Decisive Helps to Make you a Good Manager

Read any book on managerial effectiveness; listen to any lecture on managerial excellence. One thing you will find being emphasized as the top-most quality needed for a manager in all of them will be decisiveness. It is decisiveness that differentiates a professional manager from an administrator 'who somehow manages'.

Some managers may wrongly interpret this quality as if they have to be instant-solution givers when confronted with problems. When a subordinate approaches you with a complex problem and expects you to give a decision to solve it, your decision need not be an instantaneous one like pulling a magical object off your hat. Many managers lose their respect on account of their vulnerability in giving instant solutions that are either wrong, or need revision sooner.

Ingredients to good decision making

A good decision making has several ingredients like knowledge of the subject, experience, access to relevant reference data, a keen sense of judgment to pick wheat from the chaff, consulting the right persons, some amount of quality time to brood over alternatives, and a hunch feeling.

A manager, to be and become a good decision-maker, should make use of some or all of the above ingredients in a situation that demands a decision.

Consult where knowledge is lacking

A manager need not necessarily be an expert in all the areas of activity under his supervision. A good manager is one who has a good birds-eye-view of things under his command but knows where to seek advice, counsel, or direction when he is not equipped with specialized knowledge.

A manager should be open to learning and expanding his knowledge base at all times. Everyone knows that Internet is a massive storehouse of knowledge and if only you know how to search rightly through search Engines and segregate wheat from the chaff, then plenty of knowledge could be gathered from the web right from rudimentary level to expert level, if only you have time and concentration at your disposal.

A good and decisive manager does not give a wrong direction to hide his ignorance, nor does he procrastinate decision making and grope in the dark on account of his lack of knowledge. A good manager is one who has the boldness to accept his ignorance, openness to consult the right persons, and smartness to tap the right help from the right source.

A good decisive manager does not rest on his ego if he has to consult a junior who could be a specialist and the right source of knowledge. At the same time, the good decision-maker has a very strong common sense to seek the most appropriate source for guidance and adds a fair degree of his common sense, past experience, and gut feeling to weigh through the suggestions and give the right decision.

Time factor in being decisive

A good decision-maker is one who has different strategies for different situations. Where there is an emergency, he must have the swiftness to take decisions and boldness to carry them out as the situation demands. An emergency situation is not one where one has to wait for too many inputs or consult too many people. Taking calculated risks and moving ahead at speed are the requisites for a manager under such circumstances.

At another end, where there is adequate time available for decision making and the decision involves high stakes, the manager should take time to brood over the inputs and alternatives so as to arrive at the most workable and fool-proof decision. He does not unnecessarily push people around, hurry up things and end up too early to make a wrong decision.

Taking Risk is part of decisiveness

Being decisive need not mean hitting the bull's eye perfectly at all times. Good decision-making is rather a 'good batting average' in the long run. A manager, who does not have a record of a few bad decisions in his managerial capacity, may not perhaps have taken any major decision at all on his own! What's important is that the manager learns lessons from his wrong decisions and makes use of such experience in making better decisions more and more in the future.

A manager who, either on account of the mistakes he did in his decisions in the past or on account of avoiding personal risks, runs up to his boss for every petty decision that he should take at his level on his own, may perhaps please some bosses and save his skin always, but he may never become a good manager in his lifetime.

CHAPTER TWELVE

Decision Making using Weighted Average Method

Caution

In this chapter, we are going to discuss a serious and effective technique of decision making. This is not for casual reading in one go. You have to spend time to grasp the concepts, understand the nuances and calculations. Please bookmark this chapter and read it a couple of times for its contents to be digested and put to use.

Whether in business management or in personal life, we have to make decisions at several junctures. Decisiveness is a fundamental characteristic of any manager. Decision-making involves making a choice, after carefully studying the available facts, figures, and information, weighing the pros and cons, advantages and disadvantages, and then making up your mind. Some amount of influence of emotions, instincts, and a hunch feeling too cannot be ruled out in decision making.

Many times, making a choice between two seemingly "equally good" options may prove to be too daunting in decision making. Under such circumstances, the "Weighted Average Method" is a simple mathematical technique you can follow to get a clearer picture of what is a better choice.

Let us understand the whole thing through a practical example.

(1) Define your problem: Let's say you are presently employed in a firm. You are not unhappy about your position there. You have now got a new job offer with better pay, but there are several other

influencing factors to be considered over and above salary. Your problem is whether to accept the new job offer or not.

(2) List out the influencing factors: In this case, let us say these are the eight influencing factors you will consider.

(A) Location of the workplace

(B) Salary

(C) Growth prospects

(D) Matching of your qualification and experience with the job profile

(E) Your designation/ position in organizational ladder

(F) Extent of traveling involved

(G) Perks

(H) Convenient working hours (day shift / night shift)

(3) Allocate points to each of these factors in option 1 (your current job) on a 5-point scale: (i.e. give 1 point for 'least favorable'; 5 points for 'most favorable' and give 2,3,4 points suitably if your assessment is inbetween):

Your current job location is most favorable to you? Then it gets five points. Your current salary is somewhat favorable, give 3 points. Your current job involves lots of traveling that you don't really like, give 1 point. Likewise, give points for (A) to (H) in the above list.

Let's say (A) = 5, B= 3, (C) = 4, (D) = 2, (E) = 5, (F) = 1, (G) = 2, (H) = 2

Average of above = (5+3+4+2+5+1+2+2) / (8 x 5) = 24/40 = 60%

(4) Based on available information, allocate points to option 2 (your new job):

Let's say, (A) = 2, B=5, (C) = 2, (D) = 2, E = 5 (F) = 3, G = 2, (H) = 3

Average of above = (2+5+2+2+5+3+2+3) / (8 x 5) = 24/40 = 3/5 = 60%

The above is a simple average method. In this specific example, using the average method, you get same weightage for both the options and hence it will be difficult for you to come to a decision.

Now let us see how the weighted average method works.

(5) Give weightage to each of the influencing factors based on how much importance you give to each of them. Here, the 'subjective' influence (or to some extent, your emotional influence) comes into the picture at the right measure.

In doing so, the extent of compromises you are ready to make on some aspects more than some other aspects will become visible.

To understand this, let us take one aspect -- Salary. You have (as per weightage you have already given) given 3 points to it in your current job and 5 points to the new job. It obviously means the new job offers you a higher salary. Let it be.

Now, take the traveling involved in your job. You have given 1 point to your current job, while 3 points to the new job's location. It means you are more happy and comfortable with less traveling involved in the current job, than the new job.

Now between these two -- i.e salary and frequent traveling, which is subjectively more significant for you? Personally, is salary the most important? For the sake of a better salary, will you consider frequent traveling as less important?

That is the 'weightage' aspect of your decision-making.

Give weightage to each factor based on to what extent it is important to you on a 3-point scale:

* Most important for you : 3
* Moderately important to you : 2
* Least important to you : 1.

(Note: For the sake of simplicity, only a 3 point scale is suggested above. If you want, you can spread it wider like this: Least important -1, a little important -2, fairly important - 3, very important - 4, extremely important - 5. This will help you to make your decision still finer. However in this example, only a 3-point weightage is given as below).

(6) Allocate weightage: Let's say,

(A) Location: Most important for you: 3

(B) Salary level: Very much important for you: 3

(C) Growth prospects: Most Important for you: 3

(D) Matching of Qualification/ experience: Least important for you: 1

(E) Designation: Somewhat important for you: 2

(F) Traveling: You don't mind frequent traveling: 1

(G) Perks: Not too important: 2

(H) Convenient working hours: Very important for you: 3

(7) Now multiply your previously allocated points with the above weightage points:

Option: 1 - Existing job

(A) = 5x3 = 15, (B) = 3x3 = 9, (C) = 4x3 = 12, (D) = 2x1=2, (E) = 5x2 = 10 (F) = 1x1 = 1, (G) = 2x2 = 4, (H) = 2x3 = 6

Option: 2 - New Job

(A) = 2x3 = 6, (B) = 5x3 = 15, (C) = 2x3 = 6, (D) = 2x1=2, (E) = 5x2 = 10(F) = 3x1 = 3, (G) = 2x2 = 4, (H) = 3x3 = 9

(8) Now calculate the Weighted Average:

For Option: 1 - Existing Job: (15+9+12+2+10+1+4+6) / (8x5x3) = 59/120 = 49.1%

For Option: 2 - New Job: (6+15+6+2+10+3+4+9) / (8x5x3) = 55/120 = 45.8%

(9) Take the decision: Using the weighted average method, you now find that Option: 1, namely, continuing with your existing job is the better option.

What if you get the same percentage or a very narrow difference even after this exercise?

You can do the following:

Add a greater number of influencing factors. In our example, you can add: (I) Cost of living (J) Opinion of the spouse about the new job/ location (H) Reputation of the organization, (K) Scope of responsibility/ tension involved in the job, etc.

Increase the 5 point scale to, say, a 10 point scale, fine-tune the points and re-allocate them for each factor.

Increase the weightage factor from 3 to 5 (as already discussed above) and fine-tune the weightage points.

It must be remembered that no foolproof decision-making can ever be done simply based on available facts. No purely logical and objective decision can ever be made without some influence of emotions and subjectivity. The weighted average method can at the best help you in fine-tuning your decision-making process and it will be at times quite useful in justifying a decision you made!

-=()=-

CHAPTER THIRTEEN

Hidden Factors that Affect Decision making

Whether in normal life or business life, people have to make decisions in a plethora of situations and then face the consequences of those decisions. In business management, management gurus have logically earmarked steps involved in the decision-making process like defining the problem, collecting relevant data, analyzing various alternatives, consulting appropriate people, and then making up your mind on the best course of action.

But there are several hidden factors other than the above affecting the decision-making process.

Mood

The mood of a person at the juncture of making a decision is important. Where problems need instant solutions, without need or time for elaborate data collection and analysis, a manager may have to make up his mind instantaneously and it is at that juncture that moods can play a mighty swing. At times, people make quick or hasty decisions even when there is enough time and invariably, bad moods can definitely lead to wrong decisions.

Generally, if the decision-maker knows that he is emotionally surcharged and irritable, it is better that he postpones the decision-making till such time when level-headedness returns to him.

Gender of the decision-maker

It is generally perceived that men tend to make decisions more based on logic and women more based on emotions and instinct. Each approach has its positive and negative benefits. In many situations, a woman's instinct can prove to be quite right. In many situations, a man's logical decision may prove to be better than a woman's emotional decision which can be gauged by the repercussions they produce.

Bias

All of us have our own biases. Some people tend to be more biased towards people of their own religion, nationality, mother tongue, caste/ clan, region/locality, etc. Playing favoritism rather than taking a logical decision based on true merit is quite a common factor in decision-making, particularly when it comes to dealing with people.

Selfishness

Even the greatest politicians and statesmen, whom we expect to have a macro-vision and place national / people interest above anything else, tend to act extremely selfishly, when it comes to safeguarding their personal interests, reputation, or stake in a decision. Selfishness and protecting selfish interest first at the detriment of larger concerns is a common human trait that affects decision-making.

Greed

Greedy people tend to bend, break or distort rules, regulations, ethics, and decency in order to have something extra cut out for them. Receiving bribes and playing favoritism fits into this category.

Superstitions/ Astrology

Sentimental people can easily fall prey to taking illogical decisions based on superstitions or based on the counsel of what their astrologer says. A black cat crossing from left to right while one was about to call a supplier to confirm an order may trigger withholding, changing, or delaying the process of the crucial order. A businessman wanting to purchase a new Industrial Plot for his proposed factory that came at a very favorable price and locality may drop the idea of purchasing that plot if the Vastu expert says the plot has inauspicious features.

Principles and ethics

This is somewhat opposite to selfishness and greed. Some people are highly evolved in upholding ethical and moral principles and in order to uphold them, they will be prepared to incur a personal sacrifice or loss.

It is thus obvious that no decision-making can ever be impeccable with cent percent logical correctness to ensure results as expected. Every single element of extraneous factors that we discussed above can play a crucial role in the decision-making process and naturally, the outcomes too will vary accordingly.

-=()=-

CHAPTER FOURTEEN

How to be an Excellent Boss

Becoming a boss has a lot to do with what the higher-ups in management think of the potential candidate for a managerial position. But being a good boss is something to do with the subordinates. There are possibilities that a "good" manager in the eyes of the top management may turn out to be a poor boss to his subordinates.

Here are some points to ponder for any manager to become a good boss to his subordinates:

Be a Human First

A heartless taskmaster can produce excellent results that can satisfy the top management in the short run. But in the long run, such a boss may create irreparable damage to the organization from the point of view of morale and sense of belonging of the personnel to the organization. A good boss is one who has his heart too well developed along with his intellect that is task-oriented. A good boss understands the needs of catering to the family, concern for employee health, respect for employee's out-of-office interests and above all, the right amount of concern for the employees' overall wellness within and beyond office matters.

Know Your Job

A boss gets respect only if he knows his job and then commands others to do theirs. A boss is supposed to delegate work in the appropriation of the capabilities and specialties of his subordinates.

A boss who does not know his share of work nor his level of responsibility, but tends to dump them too on his subordinates so as to either enjoy his idle time or hide his ignorance is least respected.

When a subordinate comes across a genuine problem that is beyond his capacity to solve, he approaches the boss and expects him to sort it out amicably. If the boss is not immediately equipped to sort it out in his personal capacity, either he should consult those who know better or ask time to solve by suitable other means.

Any manager who brushes aside the problem as irrelevant or who misguides the subordinate on account of his ignorance can never be a good boss.

Give Credit where it is due

As a manager, the team leader is responsible for the team's performance and naturally, he gets the lion's share of the credits in the success of the team. But it should not mean that he should take the entire credit for himself by not exposing any of his stalwarts who worked hard behind the scenes. A good boss is one who brings his key subordinates into the limelight, makes sure that their individual contribution is made known to the higher echelons of management, and ensures that their career progression based on their merit is made sure through this exposure.

Don't be a bad example

A good boss is one whose conduct and character are beyond questioning. To be respected as a good boss, a manager must NOT have any of these characteristics:

- behaving indecently with employees of the opposite sex
- making calculated moves to sexually harass employees of the opposite sex by taking advantage of one's managerial power, position, or clout with the top management.
- indulging in corrupt practices with suppliers
- whiling away one's time in actively and openly engaging in office politics and nepotism
- whiling away time in the canteen or in the cabins of colleagues or subordinates just to kill time
- siphoning off office funds, perks, allowances, etc in unethical ways.

Being a good boss and becoming a respectable boss should mean one and the same. Excellence in performance with respect to the objectives set by the management can at the best be only one of many criteria to measure the goodness of a boss.

-=()=-

CHAPTER FIFTEEN

Ways to Cope with Staff who are not Productive

Just like a classroom where there will always be some dull-headed, lazy, or mischievous students, in a work team too, the presence of employees who are not productive is a reality of life. Dealing with such employees may not be a cake walk for all managers. The reasons for non-productivity could be quite wide and varying.

At times, the manager or team leader may not have all the powers and wherewithal to handle such employees singularly. He may have to work with the support of higher management in handling such issues when, in his personal capacity, he has limitations. The manager must essentially be smart enough to impartially gauge the unproductive employee's behavior, character, work ethics, and basic intelligence. At times, the very manager himself could be a potential motivator for lack of productivity in an employee!

Let us now see the various possible causes and solutions to the problems related to employees who are not productive:

The Employee having a strong clout

The inefficient or adamant employee could be the brother-in-law of the Vice President of the firm or he could have been employed by the company's proprietor because of his obligation to a major and prominent customer! The manager must be smart enough to know the background of such an employee and tread with caution. Lack of support from higher-ups in disciplining such an employee is a sure-fire indicator about the existence of the clout.

The best option for the manager is to shift the employee to less critical responsibilities and also judiciously keep his grudging colleagues informed about the power of his clout. If the manager is too smart, he can manipulate things to get the employee shifted to some other department outside his responsibility.

The general work culture and company policies about job-security

In Government employment, job security is assured in most of the countries. Even in some long-standing private organizations with a very large work force and a huge hierarchy, policies about job security are so well established that firing an employee is not easy purely based on performance grounds. Lack of threat about job security could be one of the major causes for lack of productivity in employees. But the organization may still be successful because of some innately efficient and hard working executives, who always work for the sake of their future growth either within or without the organization.

In other words, the entire organization's culture may tolerate inefficiency and mediocrity in the majority. Particularly if a new manager comes from a different organization which has a high degree of professionalism and cut-throat work culture, this "attitude" may be quite shocking. For such a person, changing the work culture requires lots of sustained effort. He has to motivate employees by personal examples of hard work and efficiency. He has to use both motivational as well as coercive techniques to change the work culture.

He needs strong support from higher-ups who believe in the need for a change. In some organizations, the inertia may be too strong that the new manager too finally loses his steam and fits himself to the 'accepted culture' of mediocrity!

Union mindset

Thanks to globalization and the gradual dying of communist ethos, the 'trade union' mentality is steadily waning across the globe. In India, members of staff who are office bearers in trade unions are of a privileged class who feel they have a fundamental right not to work! Managers normally are smart enough not to cross their way. Their lack of productivity is generally compensated by others grudgingly.

One possibility of tackling the problem is to promote such a person from the 'staff' level to 'managerial' level, subject to feasibility. The advantage is that their influence over other staff members and their 'trade union tendencies' will get curbed this way. Secondly, in most organizations, managerial inefficiency is acceptable and also taken for granted!

Work - Salary mismatch

This may happen due to the 'profit center' concept in management. Each work team will be considered as a profit center and the team leader's goal is to maximize the profits within the group. Consequently, some overzealous team leaders may overload their existing employees to cut down staff strength. Thus, limited staff may have to work overtime without proportionate compensation to complete the tasks. This may wear off employees and they may intentionally stretch the work to drive home their contention that additional hands are needed to complete the task.

In such situations, the interference from the higher management may be needed to have a balanced look at the attitude of the team leader and team's workload and wherever necessary, the team must be strengthened with additional hands or with monetary compensation for the extra workload of the existing team members.

Aging

Employees who remain in an organization for long without much growth tend to become slack; they develop certain disillusionment with the organization and its work culture. They tend to detest working under managers who are much younger and 'lack experience' from their subjective perspective. They detest any move for change from the established practices.

The solution to this problem is to treat senior and old staff with due respect for their age. They have to be frequently appreciated for their 'wisdom', knowledge about the established organizational practice, and their sense of balance. Consulting them on crucial decision-making and making them part of the decision are necessary.

Personal problems

Family problems, debts, sickness, love failure, extramarital affairs, serious conflicts with colleagues - there may be several such issues that can cause loss of productivity in an employee. "Talk to them" is the solution normally prescribed, but it may not always be easy. What if the employee does not consider his boss trustworthy enough to confide in all his personal problems and woes?

A boss can always try to initiate a dialog and if co-operation is not forthcoming, it is better to take the matter to the higher-ups. Perhaps a manager at a senior level may be found to be a better person for the staff to discuss his/her personal problems.

Thus there are myriad causes and reasons for the lack of productivity in employees. A manager has to be very shrewd as well as humane to tackle the problem according to the root cause behind it.

-=()=-

CHAPTER SIXTEEN

How to conduct a meeting

Business meetings are part and parcel of corporate life. Despite amazing improvements having taken place in instant communication systems , we still need face-to-face meetings for ensuring the most effective communication and for instilling a better sense of commitment from individuals towards goals and tasks.

Any professional manager or executive, during the course of a week, may have to conduct or participate in several meetings – intra-departmental meetings, inter-departmental meetings, meetings with higher management, meeting with customers, suppliers, and other stakeholders.

As a conductor of a meeting, you must keep in mind that any meeting consumes the time and energy of multiple people – people whose time is as valuable or perhaps more valuable than yours! In reality, you may observe that this aspect gets woefully ignored and many executives tend to utilize meetings to kill time.

Though never acknowledged, managerial idle time is a perk enjoyed by many managers and in order to hide this reality and "prove" to others that they are quite busy, many managers resort to conducting unwanted meetings! This tendency must never be emulated.

Here are some tips for conducting effective and

productive meetings:

Be clear about the agenda

Everyone attending a meeting should be clear about the agenda of the meeting. Members should come to the meeting well-prepared beforehand, and the meeting should not be allowed to drift to free-wheeling discussions on unrelated topics.

Involve only those who are concerned

Many professional managers take pride in being the chairperson of the meeting attended by all irrespective of whether the attendants have something to contribute or otherwise – in other words, conducting a meeting more as a ritual for the pride of doing it.

For example, in a meeting to discuss the frequent breakdown of a critical machine and the consequential loss of production, the role of a Marketing Executive will be nil. But he may have been asked to attend it as a 'ritual'. Such practices are to be abhorred.

Relieve early those who have contributed

In a meeting with multiple agendas, perhaps some of the participants have very little to say or contribute and they have already said it. It will be a criminal waste of their time to retain them till the end of the meeting; they will be sitting there uselessly, yawning and squirming in their seats or scribbling your caricature in their writing pads! It is in the best interest of all that those who have contributed already in the meeting are allowed to leave early.

Be focused

Go prepared with a check-list of matters to be discussed in the meeting. Smart executives on the receiving end (who are likely to face the wrath from fellow members in the meeting on account of their omissions and commissions) have the knack of diverting the focus of the meetings to non-issues; they will smartly try to steer away from the discussions to irrelevant issues in order to wriggle out of their predicaments. You must be constantly watchful of such persons; remain in control to prevent such diversionary tactics and steer the focus of the discussions to subjects in the agenda.

Meetings are not just for monolog

Occasionally, meetings are conducted for making announcements only (policy announcements, announcements about promotions, new product launches, felicitation to a retiring staff member, etc). Other than such cases, if you are conducting a meeting just for the love of 'hearing your own voice', just to make your sermons and expect others to listen, nod, and leave, the meeting hardly serves any purpose. A meeting should be ideally for open discussions. Every member in a meeting should have the opportunity to express himself unreservedly. Listening and talking should be roughly equal.

Ensure everybody contributes

This is particularly important in the case of brainstorming sessions. Any meeting will consist of a few over-talkative persons, some who have the capacity to express themselves well and some who are reserved, shy to talk, having limitations in verbal expressiveness. Many times, shy and reserved persons will have more creativity and better ideas than those who have the capacity of stronger vocal cords. This is where your capacity as the organizer of an effective meeting is put to test. You have to cajole and encourage the shy and reserved persons to come out of their shells and contribute their might well, and by keeping a check on the over-talkative persons.

Decide on who-what-when

Whether it is problem-solving or allocating new tasks, you should clearly communicate in the meeting on WHO should do WHAT within what TIME FRAME without ambiguity. All the concerned members must be clear of their roles and responsibilities and have their concurrence.

Summarize and make them committed

If a meeting is a routine and ongoing one (daily production meetings, weekly sales meetings, etc), start off with the gist of points concluded in the last meeting and check to see compliance and deviations.

Every member who has to do his role of follow-up action after the meeting is over must be asked to jot down what he has committed to do, and what he ought to do along with the time frame in his notepad. You must also jot down in your own way these commitments in your notepad, which will serve you as the basis for follow-up. This is a simpler alternative to making "official minutes".

At the end of the present meeting, summarize the key points discussed and agreed upon before dispersing.

Make official minutes where it is a must

In very crucial meetings, it will be necessary to make written official minutes that record the gist of discussions and outline the action plan covering "who-what-when". Here are some of the possible conditions that make minutes essential:

- The summary of discussions is to be sent to higher-ups for further action.
- The meeting is between a customer and a supplier and it covers action plans related to a tender; finalization of Order; problems in sales and service; payment and delivery commitments; and

trials and quality issues, etc.

- The meeting is a brainstorming session and all the ideas and points of view generated are to be made available in an organized way.

Be time-conscious

Start the meeting in time and conclude it in time. Do not stretch the meeting by 'eating' away lunchtime! Some executives conduct meetings intentionally beyond office hours, which is blatantly an undesirable practice.

* * *

Managerial effectiveness many times gets reflected in the effectiveness of the meetings one conducts. Meetings should never be used as a time-pass by a manager to camouflage his idle time. If a meeting with multiple persons can effectively be avoided by any other means of efficient communication, it would definitely be a more worthwhile effort on the part of the manager towards effective time management.

-=()=-

CHAPTER SEVENTEEN

Why Good Bosses don't Flaunt their Power

When power is given, two basic human tendencies are difficult to resist: one to misuse the power and the other to flaunt it. When a boss occasionally misuses his power, he may get away with it; when the boss frequently misuses his power, he may get caught one day. But when he flaunts his power, he loses nothing imminently, except perhaps his respectability in the eyes of his subordinates.

A boss' power comes in several forms that include his power to hire and fire, to spend the organization's money within certain limits and at times beyond it, his clout and capacity to heavily influence the higher echelons of management, his political connections (if any), his capacity to influence the police/ law enforcing agencies, etc.

A good boss makes use of whatever powers under his command for carrying out his duties and responsibilities to the organization. A good boss is one who is self-sure about his capacities and capabilities. By virtue of his efficiency in carrying out his duties and tasks, he commands respect from those who work under him. He does not feel the need to flaunt his power to his subordinates to prove his stature and position in the organization.

In contrast, what is it that makes a boss flaunt his power in front of others, particularly to his subordinates? There could be several causes for it and almost all of them can be traced to the inherent weaknesses that he wants to conceal. What are they?

Desire to show off

A boss who thinks that an occasional self-boasting or a demonstration of his powers is quite justified for having risen to such a prestigious level in the organization, with his dubious credentials.

Sexual Promiscuity

Bosses with fundamentally weak ethics and morality particularly in matters related to sex, might feel tempted to flaunt their power to lure meek subordinates of the opposite sex. While some bosses might even taste success in their nefarious moves initially, such a behavior is sure to bring doom to his career sooner or later.

Worry about loss of respect

A boss with limitations in managerial capabilities, self-confidence, and intelligence resorts to flaunting his power with the intent to somehow garner respectability.

Worry about smarter subordinates

A boss who feels threatened by very smart subordinates working under him may feel his position is shaky. So he flaunts his power with the hope that the smarter subordinates don't end up playing mischief against him.

Worry about exposure of misdeeds

A boss' nefarious activities done against the interests of the organization may have become known to some of his key subordinates and the subordinates may have made their objections known to the boss on such activities. To keep their mouths shut, the boss may flaunt his power to threaten them to silence.

Obviously, a truly good boss is one who does not fit into these situations, and naturally, he won't have the need to flaunt his power.

-=()=-

CHAPTER EIGHTEEN

Warning Signals to know you are going to get fired from your Job

If you are attentive enough, you can hear distant rumblings of thunder before dark clouds reach above your head to bring rain. Likewise, if you are watchful enough, you can definitely pick up disturbing signals to alert you if you are going to be fired from the job.

Getting fired from the job can be en masse at times. A severe recession, a major loss in the company, a dire need for downsizing for the sake of business survival, shifting of operations to a distant land for the sake of economics -- there could be several reasons for you to get fired along with several of your colleagues, subordinates and supervisors.

Or you may get fired all alone, on account of your omissions and commissions or inefficiency.

In case the firing is going to take place en masse -- a retrenchment, here are some warning signals:

Rumors

When a company is really in bad shape and there are rumors floating around that there are going to be job-cuts, do not ignore the rumors lightly, even if your company's official spokesman says the rumors are baseless! Smoke will not come without fire. Unless some talk has taken place at higher echelons of management about the likelihood of effecting job cuts, rumors will not be floating around.

Some management may even intentionally float the rumor and deny it; it's a way of creating the 'right atmosphere' for declaring the bad news at a later date!

Serious economy measures

The penultimate step before doing job cuts could be in the form of cuts in salaries, perks, allowances, free supplies (like uniform, office stationery, coffee/tea/snacks) etc. If you have taken some advances, you will get a notice to repay them earlier than scheduled. Short lay-off coupled with pay cuts may become frequent. Those who submit resignations will be found relieved immediately without waiting for the customary ending of the notice period.

The management's tactics and moves will look as though they encourage employees to quit and leave the company, however important their position might have been in the past.

Kindness

The immediate manager may suddenly start behaving too humanely and kindly to his subordinates who are on the firing list. He may start showing keen interest in the family and well being of the employees!

If you are going to get fired alone, on account of real or perceived omissions and commissions, look for the following signals:

Irritable and never-satisfied boss

Your boss will start picking holes in whatever work you do; he will shout at you for petty reasons; he will constantly show displeasure at your lack of performance and your incapacity to learn and grow.

Coldness/ sidelining

Your boss may become too cold with you. He may avoid meeting you and giving you guidance on your on-job doubts and problems. He may stop giving you promised assignments and responsibilities and divert them to a colleague to handle them as additional responsibilities. When you are desperately in need of help on the job, your boss, who would have given you guidance in the past under similar circumstances, will now direct one of your senior colleagues to give you instructions.

Important meetings in which you were normally a part in the past will now be conducted without inviting you. Important e-mail communications which were usually copied to you will not be reaching you now. Some of your subordinates will be getting instructions directly from the big boss and they will try to avoid keeping you informed.

Weird behavior of colleagues

If you are going to get fired alone, it is a strange reality that the rumor mill will start working absolutely behind your back, without the news reaching up to your ears! Some of your colleagues may perhaps know about your fate already, but they will not reveal it to you. They will start distancing from you and avoid mingling with you during lunchtime or in the canteen.

Some of your juniors suddenly may show a callous attitude towards you and a sense of respect or restraint seen earlier may be missing.

Getting "kicked up" as a prelude to getting "kicked out"

Kicking-up means a dubious promotion. A promotion, really? Yes. Strange it may look, but it is another dirty tactic played by some top management. Suppose you have served an organization for quite a long, but somehow, currently your position has become redundant in the organization. It may happen on account of several reasons - your age and related arrival of inefficiency and lethargy, your specialty skills getting outdated, your attitude of "taking the company for granted", your constant criticism about new managerial policies being contradictory to "time tested" and old practices, your dislike towards your new and much younger boss, etc.

By way of respect to your long service in the company, the management may not want to get rid of you the harsh way. So, they would move you out of the mainline of activity by giving you a "promotion" and shift you to the new post and place. While you gleefully accept the new position considering that it is an elevation in recognition of your services, it will virtually be the death trap for your career in the organization!

The new post will have no clearly defined responsibilities; you won't have any people to manage, but you may have to "coordinate" with many other managers who will not report to you (nor respect you) to carry out your unclear tasks! You will be given a cabin in a secluded corner of the building and you won't have a Personal Secretary now, if you had one earlier.

None of your former colleagues will have time to spend with you. None of your erstwhile subordinates will give respect to you. You will collect your monthly salary for doing nothing and no one in the top echelons of management will bother about your existence, except perhaps for laughing at you behind your back.

If you are a sensitive person, you will quit on your own and that's precisely what the top management wants. If you are too thick-skinned, perhaps you will get kicked out in due course and the management will give enough good reasons by pointing out your lack of contribution to the organization in your current post!

-=()=-

CHAPTER NINETEEN

How to know when You're being Overworked

When you are being overworked, it may be due to two reasons – one, you are doing so on account of loving your job too much and two, you are forced to work out of compulsion, without your conscious willingness. The symptoms of being overworked will vary depending on these two.

If you overwork because you have fallen in love with your work, here are some symptoms:

Obsessiveness

You will ignore your sleep, your food, your responsibilities at home and you will be constantly engrossed in your job. Unless someone reminds you or forces you to go home, you would rather go ahead with your job on hand. Worse still, you will expect those who work under you too to emulate you; you will consider hardwork as the greatest virtue. Even if you sleep, you will go to bed with the thoughts and plans related to your work and when you wake up, you will emerge with the same thoughts.

Your work will not look boring to you. You will get offended if your spouse or someone makes fun of your obsessiveness. You will feel proud of your dedication and sincerity.

Neglecting dear ones

Spending quality time with your spouse or children will never be a matter of importance to you. If your spouse complains loudly, you will declare that your first love is your job and everything else is secondary. If the family emotionally blackmails you, you too will become emotional to highlight how important your work is to you and you will end up saying that you are toiling day and night just to ensure the happy well-being of the family in the long run. You will declare that the family should sacrifice short-term pleasures for the sake of your long-term success!

Ignoring physical ailments

Your body may resist abuse and over-stretching and it may react; you may get physical fatigue, dizziness, acidity, headache, cough and cold, body aches, and so on. But your tendency would be to ignore them and keep moving ahead with your work, till your physical ailments lead you to a body breakdown.

Now let us see some symptoms of overworking on account of compulsion:

Irritability

You will become short-tempered. You may shout at your subordinates; you may enter into unnecessary arguments with your colleagues. Your children will feel afraid of coming closer to you when you return home. You will use your spouse and children as 'emotional toilets' to vent your frustration at the workplace. Bickering and fighting with the spouse will be routine affairs. Sexual relationship with the partner will deteriorate.

Fatigue

You will feel too tired most of the time. You would like to get uninterrupted, peaceful sleep for at least seven to eight hours at a stretch, but you will find it extremely difficult to fall asleep; you will be consciously aware of your tossing and turning at the bed right through your sleeping hours.

You will dream of obsessively working on a trivial job repeatedly again and again, but neither completing it nor getting it right.

Inefficiency

You will be pumping in more and more working hours with less and less efficiency. You will get dissatisfied with your own output and your inability to do things right the first time. You will find that your concentration is lacking and in order to get it, you will think of diverting your time to something else for a while (chit-chatting with your friends, browsing the internet, visiting the canteen, going out for frequent smoking, etc). When you return to resume your work, you will find yourself in no way better.

You will always find yourself not having enough time in a day. The more you work, the more you will find your work stretching.

Complaining

You will be regularly complaining about something to somebody. "It's a thankless job; the boss takes all the credit for my toil; the boys working under me never take responsibility; I have a terrible headache all through the day; I hate going home; my wife is a torture....."

Real and imagined ailments

Headache, back pain, dizziness, vomiting sensation, indigestion, insomnia, ulcer, fever – you may frequently get these ailments, and even if they are not, you will keep complaining about such ailments.

Smoking and drinking

Excessive smoking, indulgence in alcoholic drinks, eating junk food at odd times – these too are some of the symptoms of overworking.

Whether one works out of obsession for the job or out of fear about job security, being overworked has the potential to damage one's physical and mental health in the long run. Whether work, play, food, sleep, or sex, everything in life has to have a degree of moderation and that's the secret of leading a successful and happy life in this world.

Gossips in the office

An idle mind is the workshop of the devil. If gossiping in the office is widespread, there are two causes: One employee idleness and two, managerial idleness.

Surprisingly, many managers and supervisors indulge in gossip inside the office, not necessarily with their staff, but more likely with their peers and colleagues. Managerial idleness is one of the prime causes for it. A manager, after delegating work and conducting useful and useless meetings, if still left with nothing more to do, goes from cabin to cabin to engage in idle talk with other idle (or busy) managers, to kill time. This exercise includes plenty of gossiping.

When managers are found whiling away their time in idle talk, the staff members also get enthused to emulate their bosses.

How to stop such unwanted and harmful gossip taking place around the office?

Attention Top management: Avoid managerial idleness

As said in the beginning, managerial idleness is one of the causes for gossip and rumor-mongering. Many times, promotions are given to staff as a reward for their hard work, but at no point in time, the proportion of managers should be unnecessarily more than the staff strength that they are supposed to supervise. This has to be ensured by the top management. Managers are to be allotted with work and responsibilities that they should perform in their individual capacity other than those that they are supposed to delegate.

Keep the staff engaged

Do not allow free time or idle time to the staff. Keep loading them with work; if there are not enough tasks to be carried out currently, engage them in futuristic tasks or engage them in housekeeping.

Let the bug stop at you

If the office is gossiping about a possible shakeout in the top management and they come to you seeking any juicy tidbits, stoutly deny any knowledge of such matters and ask them to concentrate on their work. Do not knowingly or unknowingly participate in their discussions and make yourself vulnerable to gossiping behavior.

Increase the male to female ratio

Women are more prone to gossiping. When the staff strength of the fairer sex is more, a good suggestion is to reduce the female population in group tasks and increase the male population.

Nip in the bud

If any strong rumors or gossip are afloat about any indecent behavior between specific male and female members in the office, make sure whether any such behavior is really true and if so, call the concerned persons and issue veiled warnings. Or, if your position is not strong enough to take such an action, bring it to the notice of higher management.

Gossip and rumor-mongering, if left unchecked, will gradually spread like a contagious disease and gobble up productive hours in the office. Management should assiduously avoid such a thing happening inside the office.

-=()=-

CHAPTER TWENTY-ONE

Why don't more People Pursue their Dream Job

A dream job is one where your educational qualification, expertise and past experience match very well with your job profile; your salary and perks are the best, commensurate with some or all the above aspects; your temperament and the organization's working culture are in sync; you have a boss with common-sense whose frequency matches with yours; you are able to spare time after office hours to spend with your family and pursue your interest and hobbies; your job security and future growth are comfortably and reasonably assured.

Well, getting most or all the above can perhaps happen in your dream or in the heavens!

In reality, our expectations on our job may be disproportionately higher than our true worth; we generally tend to rate ourselves at a position far above in a scale than what we truly deserve. The economic scenario, trends in the market, rapid changes in technology, macro level Government policies, family pulls and pressures - there are umpteen factors that have their influence in our getting, fitting in or pursuing our dream jobs.

Salary

If you look for one top-most factor that decides against our fitting into a dream job, it is salary. A couple of years back, in India, the IT boom was at its peak. Engineering degrees in Computer science, Information Technology, Electronics and communication etc were the most sought after ones because in these segments, the job openings were plenty and the salaries offered were far above the other branches of core engineering lines like mechanical engineering or civil engineering.

The demand in the job market for IT-oriented openings were so large that there was actually a shortage of manpower and IT firms freely recruited engineering graduates from other streams of engineering like mechanical, electrical and electronics and so on for IT jobs (and trained them up). The salaries offered to such engineers were again in tune with the IT Industry and core industries in these segments could hardly match these salaries.

Result? Many engineering graduates, who studied mechanical engineering and the like, who had lots of aspirations to progress in their core lines (their dream jobs) ended up joining the IT Industry for the simple reason that the salaries offered to them were so high!

Commitments

Amidst married couples, sometimes the husband or wife may have to compromise from chasing their dream jobs for the sake of being together in one place; sometimes commitments towards children (children's health, education etc) will force people from chasing their dream jobs.

Misplaced expectations

Sometimes, a job that one previously held will suddenly turn out to be a dream job and the reality will hit the face only after switching over to a new job! How? Looking for greener patches, a person may switch to a new job where his past qualifications, experience, nature of responsibility and so on may fit beautifully well along with a big chunk of increase in salary; but he may find belatedly that the new organization's work culture, the camaraderie between staff, colleagues and the boss, freedom of working, the convenience of working hours and many such things were far better in his previous job; he may even feel that the satisfaction of the pay increase was no compensation for all those things that he had enjoyed previously.

Life cannot be led successfully without compromises. Not pursuing one's dream job will also be one such compromise in many people's lives.

-=()=-

CHAPTER TWENTY-TWO

Understanding and tackling Procrastination

(**Note**: *This chapter has been intentionally written on a lighter note, for a change!*)

    * * *

I was planning to write on this topic for the past one month, but somehow kept on postponing it.

"Why?" you may ask; "Were you too busy in your other pressing activities?"

Sorry! If I were really too busy on something else to take up writing on this topic, I can't call it procrastination.

"Perhaps you could not get enough ideas to write the article or to organize the ideas properly to present it neatly?"

Maybe yes; maybe no. I had some half-baked ideas alright; At the back of my mind I was also thinking about how to organize the ideas in a presentable form; otherwise, why should I still be interested in writing on this subject? Actually, I was feeling sort of...

"Lazy?"

Mmmmm....maybe yes; maybe no. What I am trying to say is...

"There was not enough motivation to write the article? Perhaps you would have done it if there were some tangible benefits to enthuse you?"

You can say so; Maybe you are right, but that's not the thing. Why? Yesterday, I fixed the problem in the switchboard in the bathroom water-heater; my wife had been complaining about it for the past 3 weeks; Yesterday, she started yelling at me and I left everything else to do it. There is no reward in doing it, you see?

"Ah! Now I understand! Even if you are not motivated by rewards, you take up a long-neglected work if somebody reprimands you!"

No, no! Do you mean to say I am afraid of my wife? Never. It's just that the complaint was genuine and, after all, I knew I can fix it myself without calling an electrician.

"Then why didn't you do it 3 weeks ago when your wife pointed out the problem to you?"

I was busy mentally thinking about writing this article you know! Okay; okay. You don't believe it; leave it. Don't think I am a habitual procrastinator. When my boss wanted me to finish and submit the Sales Projection report for the next quarter before the last Month-end deadline, I did it! I burnt my midnight oil on the previous night to finish the report sharp on the 1st. See?

"I understand. You require a deadline, that too, to be set by an authority whom you can't disobey..."

In this case, you can say so. But two months back, the same boss asked me to complete a profit-loss statement for a specific product line that we are manufacturing. I am yet to submit it; I am not overly concerned about his questioning about it; he hasn't asked me so far. See? Don't think I am of the type who keeps his tails between the hind legs and runs at the sight of the boss.

"That's interesting! How come you could get away with that?"

The fact is, it is not actually my job. It was supposed to be done by the specific Works Manager in charge of the product line. The Works Manager does not report to my boss and he cares the least about the useless statistics the marketing department keeps demanding! So, my boss passed the bug to me. Why should I do it? It's not my baby!

"But what if your boss demands it from you by exercising his authority?"

Let me do it at that point of time. Till then I have the pleasure of procrastinating!

"I think you have gathered practically all the points you require to write an article about procrastination by now! How about doing it right now?"

No. I am not in a mood. Somehow, for the past 1 week, I feel somewhat dull, lethargic, drained out. I am also oversleeping a bit. I don't know why. I don't think I am sick. Perhaps, there is some nutritional imbalance. Maybe there is a shortage of Vitamin B in my food intake. Maybe it's because of climate change. I hope it's a temporary phenomenon. At times it happens to everybody, you know. I will do it; I will definitely write the article.

"Perhaps if your wife shouts at you?"

You are crossing the limits. Goodbye.

-=()=-

CHAPTER TWENTY-THREE

How Professional Values and Ethics can Impact on Career Success

There are some people, particularly among businessmen, who say that personal principles, values and ethics should not be meddled with in business dealings. There is a saying in Tamil to support this line of argument which suggests "money got by selling a dog doesn't bark and the money got by selling fish doesn't stink". But in the long run, if a businessman or an executive wants real peace of mind, stability in business/career and a sense of self-fulfillment in career or life, he cannot afford to divorce ethics from business.

In a highly competitive business environment, business interests and professional ethics may cross the path of each other quite frequently. Temptations to "somehow" clinch a golden business opportunity by sidelining ethics and principles may come at several occasions in business life. Paying bribes, receiving bribes, supplying sub-standard quality, creating artificial scarcity, making false promises about delivery, doing adulteration of materials, tax evasion - there are umpteen possibilities in business to sideline ethics so as to make a quick buck in the short run.

It is quite possible to make filthy profits in the short run through filthy business practices. As long as the unethical business practices go on stealthily, one may happily indulge in such practices, but if the transactions get exposed, the business may get blacklisted by the buyers. Some unethical practices like adulteration, cheating in the quantity of supply, weight, etc, if caught red-handed, can even put the business owner behind the bars. Any bad name obtained by a business house takes quite a long time to repair and it is not easy to regain customer confidence.

On the other hand, good principles and values followed in the business may even impact adversely on profitability in the short run. But short-sightedness in business can never bring respectability and prestige to the business owners or to the business executives in society.

Another important practical reality any executive must be aware of is the attitude of business owners, who mostly sit on the fence when it comes to professional values and ethics. An over-smart business executive may happily indulge in business practices aimed at maximizing profits for the company by neglecting ethics and principles. As long as things go on smoothly without any hiccups, the business owners will turn a blind eye to the executive's questionable practices; the executive may even get quick promotions and financial rewards in appreciation of his contribution.

But should something go wrong and the organization ends up in a difficult position (a business scam, a journalistic exposure about high-level corruption, unfair and antisocial trade practices, etc) the owners or the top management will make the same executive, whom they have been nurturing all along, a scapegoat. From floating in cloud nine, the executive's career may take a nosedive and crash into troubled waters. Short-term successes cannot guarantee a steady career if professional ethics and values are sidelined.

It is an obvious conclusion - whether one is a businessman or an executive concerned about his career in the organization, professional values and ethics are a must for success in the long run.

-=()=-

CHAPTER TWENTY-FOUR

How Spirituality can Lead you to a different and Rewarding Career

Work as well as career has a tendency to bind people. People get bound to their careers for the sake of money, power, and prestige. Aspiration for more money, power, and position grows into ambition and if left unchecked, into obsession and greed.

When people find less scope for growth in all of these spheres in one job, they go in pursuit of a career change in order to satiate their ever-growing ambitions. The moment one starts getting propelled by ambition and greed, one loses mental peace and balance. His spiritual being gets disturbed. Anxiety to win and stress to prove himself better than competing colleagues set in.

Understanding Conflicting Pairs Of Opposites

Unfortunately, gain and loss, pleasure and pain, success and failure, jubilation and depression - all such pairs of opposites seem to come together like the two sides of the same coin. Most people are not sensitive enough to grasp this divine dispensation and they madly go behind their quest for success, mostly without much moral balance, hoping in vain that they can fight out to win the positive half without the need to bear the negative half, by driving themselves ambitiously.

However, some people, at some point of time in life, get awakened to the reality that no long-lasting happiness, satisfaction, or fulfillment is attained through mad pursuits behind money, wealth, power, position, fame, or authority. They could get this feeling through bitter personal experiences, or by observing the rise and fall of so-called successful people in life, or through the holy association with saints.

When this reality dawns, the mind turns towards spirituality to find a possible solution to acquiring more of the beneficial side with less of the contradicting side in the above-listed pairs of opposites.

Spirituality and Discrimination

A person, thus far running his life from an ego-centric level, turns towards a God-centric mindset, through properly understood spirituality. A rightly tuned spiritual mind makes one understand that most of the things happening in life are through a hidden divine dispensation. The more one takes action based on unbridled desires and ego-centric cravings, the more trouble one gets into.

Not everyone who turns spiritual can become a saint. Most of the spiritually inclined persons, who have to lead a worldly life and earn money for nurturing themselves and their family, can definitely gain discrimination - a better psychic ability to discern good from bad, right from the wrong, healthy from the unhealthy, legal from the illegal, moral from the immoral, permanent from the transient.

When discrimination dawns, people can re-tune their mindset from pursuing transient worldly success to attaining long-lasting peace and a sense of fulfillment in their lives.

Morality and Career

No spiritual progress is ever possible without the right moral conduct. This is fundamental in any religion. As in personal life, the need for adhering to moral values is essential in career progress too. This fact is not understood by many.

People who have faced career upheavals and have fortunately turned to spirituality can understand the above fact better. It can lead one to a career change and such a change can greatly lessen the negatives and mental conflicts faced earlier.

Let us see a couple of practical examples.

Real-life example 1

A Sales Executive, engaged in selling office equipment and consumables, was brought up by spiritually inclined parents with a mindset that selling something by corrupt means is essentially wrong. But in his present career, his company expects him to sell their sub-standard products to Government departments by bribing the officials. He is constantly in a dilemma about playing such a role. Because of this inner conflict, he is not successful in his career in comparison with his colleagues and his career growth is in jeopardy.

He comes across a vacancy in the company for the post of Logistics Executive (a job involving products distribution and delivery, which does not involve any direct selling to customers). He convinces the management to shift him to that post. He regains his mental peace and is able to perform his new role well, to the satisfaction of his company.

Real-life example 2

A Manufacturing manager experienced in pharmaceutical products joins a new company that offers him a hefty 40% pay hike when compared to his previous job. He is put in charge of selecting plant and machinery for the manufacture of Intravenous fluids, a new product line for the company. One of the sellers offers second-hand Plant and Machinery at a very attractive price and offers to pay a hefty bribe to him. He gets tempted and recommends procurement of the plant from this source.

After the plant is commissioned and the first batch of IV fluids sold, the marketing department starts receiving complaints that the presence of fungus is noticed by hospitals in their samples. Several lots get rejected.

The management wants the Manufacturing Manager to technically solve the problem. He spends several sleepless nights redesigning, modifying, and refurbishing the equipment, but none of his attempts becomes successful. Based on his advice, the company continues with manufacturing and marketing the IV fluids and opts to give free replacements or bribes to those customers who complain about the fungus problem in the IV Sachets.

One day, the son of the manager meets with an accident and gets hospitalized in a serious condition. The manager is shocked to find that the IV fluid administered to his son is of his own company's make. He spends a sleepless night worrying about its impact on his son's health. Now, the Manager's conscience pricks him to no end.

He starts spiritual self-inquiry and feels his son's predicament is a consequence of his moral lapse at his company. He makes an appointment with his previous employer who shows a willingness to take him back, but only at his previously paid salary level. The manager accepts the offer. He feels a great sense of relief now.

Certain professions are inherently more susceptible to moral conflicts for those who have spiritual moorings in them. Examples are police, criminal lawyers, politicians, sellers of arms and ammunition, sellers of tobacco-based or narcotic products, and so on. For those who get troubled by conscience, spirituality can help them to change their career to get better peace of mind and tranquility in life.

Part B

Survival and success guide

for the salaried executive

== At Home ==

How is it possible for an Individual to Successfully Preserve Balance in their life?

What is a balanced life?

A life where ups and downs are minimal, emotional swings are not too fast, joys and sorrows are less alternating, and above all, peace rather than peaks and troughs is more prevalent.

After spending considerable years in life in search of money, position, power, status, conjugal bliss, and so on, many a time we end up with a feeling that in the bargain, we have lost balance in life. Many of us do not know that having mental peace itself could be a worthwhile goal in our life and we can work our way to attain it! It would be even better if we develop such a mindset early in life.

Life essentially consists of certain ways and means within our control and certain happenings and circumstances beyond our control. By acting on those within our control we can strive for leading a peaceful and balanced life. A spiritual and philosophical mindset would add fillip to our efforts.

Here are some steps to lead a balanced life:

1. Have a clearcut self-judgment about your true capabilities, strengths, and limitations

You might possess excellent Soccer skills within your local league. But it need not mean you are competent enough to play for the national team. Compare yourself with better players and make a sincere judgment: Do I really play or am I capable of playing to that level? Do I have the physical, psychological and financial resources to make myself fit enough to come up to that level? Above all, is such a yearning worth the effort?'

Sheer positive thinking alone will not do wonders. In the scheme of nature, all are not endowed with the same set of skills and resources. If you are capable of judging yourself correctly, you will be endowed with peace of mind by not pursuing something beyond your reach.

2. Do not compare yourself with others

Your life is your own. Your likes and dislikes, tastes, expectations, and standards are your own. Your neighbor or your colleague need not be a benchmark for you to compare yourself or compete with. Their level of education, financial status, social status, or spending pattern need not be yours. If at all you have to compare, compare yourself with those who are less privileged than you; those whose lives are more peaceful and less complicated than yours.

3. Do not aspire to make others' dream your reality

Your father's unfulfilled dream of becoming a doctor need not be your dream. Your mother's dream of becoming a successful dancer need not be yours unless and until you, on your own uninfluenced self-judgment, think the same way.

4. Never get addicted to anything

Be it, drinking, smoking, sex, profession, money, fame, or recognition, moderation is the key to a peaceful life. Eat moderately. Sleep moderately. Work moderately. Have sex moderately. Do not stretch yourself beyond limits.

5. Live within your means

This is time-tested, age-old wisdom that is unfortunately forgotten in today's Credit Card culture. What you buy using a Credit Card should be payable IN FULL by you when the bill arrives from the Credit Card firm. If you get lured by the "Minimum Amount due Now", it paves the way for accumulation of debt and consequently loss of peace sooner or later. If the object of desire can be purchased by you only through Installment by utilizing the "Minimum Payout Money", DO NOT SUCCUMB to the temptation of purchase. By bringing in this self-control, you may lose short-term pleasures, but you will enjoy long-term peace.

Procurement of Capital intensive items like a Flat/ house should be strictly within your well-thought-out budgets, taking into account your repaying capacity under realistic situations and NOT based on your dreams of making a big fortune in your future endeavors.

6. Regularly save a percentage of your income

At any point in time, should you come across a bad patch in life like losing a job or a loss in your business, etc., you should be in a position to pull along comfortably at least for a few months on the strength of your savings.

7. Run around less

Avoid unnecessary travel. Communicate better and more effectively through the various avenues and media so that personal face-to-face meetings by traveling long distances can be reduced.

Delegate more. Remember that traveling long distances taxes your health by upsetting and altering your eating and sleeping rhythms, which in turn affect your peace of mind.

8. Intentionally slow down

Don't madly run behind high targets and goals. Reduce your standards of expectation from others. If you are running, switch over to walking! Remember: You don't really have any obligation to prove anything about yourself to others! Perhaps you may even be better off by extending the principle that you don't really have to prove anything about yourself to yourself too, if you can!

9. Let the wellness of your family take precedence over your profession

Remember: The fundamental needs of any human being are rather simple and basic: Good food, good clothing, and a good shelter. Under shelter comes the family. When you have a good conjugal relationship, nice children, healthy homely food, and the loving embrace of the beloved ones' arms when you are physically or mentally down, you have mostly got what is fundamentally essential for peace. Any other pursuit that goes against these and disturbs these fundamentals will only add to your misery.

10. Avoid poking your nose unnecessarily into others' affairs

Extend a helping hand to others, within your capacity and limits when help is sought from you. Do not over-stretch yourself in helping others and get into trouble. Being over-willing to help may invariably end up in one being taken undue advantage of. Also, do not offer help with a calculative mind to get something in return in the future. Helping others willingly is of course a spiritual quality but it requires a spiritually cultivated mind to handle the repercussions peacefully.

11. Be health-conscious, but don't make a fetish about your health

By eating in time, eating moderately, eating nutritious food and by exercising moderately, keep your physical health fit. Do not read beyond rudimentary facts about various ailments, their symptoms and their cure! Excessive knowledge about various ailments will add to wild imagination about their existence in your body!

12. Live within the moral frameworks acceptable to the elders in the society

Every new generation makes a compromise in moral standards of the previous generation and dilutes them to a lower level. Moral laxity is conducive for instant gratification and unbridled thrills but a sure ingredient for loss of peace. Sticking to moral standards set by morally sound elders of the previous generations is a trait you can follow to lead a peaceful life.

13. Watch your ego

The formula is very simple. The extent of your egotism is directly proportional to the loss of mental peace! Are you over-sensitive? Do you put your self-interest always by bulldozing others' rightful share? Consciously analyze such traits in you and make a sincere attempt to straighten yourself.

14. Have faith in the higher power governing all

Have faith in God. Always remember that you are mostly a puppet in the hands of a higher power whose scheme of things is mostly beyond human comprehension. Surrender to that force. Accept and be content about the cards you have received and play with the best of your ability using the cards available in your hands. Accept with humility the outcome of the game.

-=()=-

CHAPTER TWENTY-SIX

Top 10 Simple Ways to Stay Fit

Staying fit is generally associated with physical well-being. But it should rightfully extend to mental well being too, as the condition of the human body is intrinsically connected to the state of mind as well. Here are 10 simple prescriptions for ways to stay fit.

1. Eat moderately

Never eat to your stomach's full capacity. The Indian system of healthy eating recommends that you eat only half to two-thirds of your stomach's capacity. The rest of the space in the stomach is to be left for consuming water and to allow the gasses released in the process of digestion to find space and escape comfortably.

Where one is used to eating heavily all along, one may initially find it very difficult to curtail eating to this specification. But by persistent practice, one will find that the stomach shrinks to a lesser size over a period of time and the body gets tuned to this healthy habit.

2. Eat in time, eat as per the ancient wisdom

I do not prescribe to the present day-view that one's food intake should be split into smaller intakes to be consumed 5 to 6 times a day. I recommend, based on personal experience, that the traditional practice of taking 3-meals a day -- the breakfast in the morning (around 8:00-9:00 AM), the lunch (around 1:00 to 2:00 PM), and dinner (around 7:30 to 8:30 PM) is the best for a healthy living.

The ancient wisdom also states that the breakfast must be sumptuous, the lunch moderate, and the dinner, meager. As the stomach remains empty over the night, it has the capacity to digest the sumptuous breakfast most efficiently and quickly. The lunch sustains the energy needs for the day and the meager dinner is good enough for a peaceful night's sleep.

Avoid drinking coffee or tea in-between meal times unnecessarily. Do not eat any snacks in between; even if you eat, make sure that the stomach is fully empty before you consume the next meal.

Drink plenty of water right through the day. In the morning after brushing teeth, drinking a large cup of water is recommended, which does the first cleansing of the digestive system for the day.

3. Eat balanced food

Though it may not be practicable for all, taking vegetarian food definitely adds to healthy living in the long run. In your vegetarian food, make sure that your food intake is well balanced with cereals, pulses, vegetables, fruits, greens, moderate amounts of fat, sweets, milk, and milk products. It is always best to go by the traditional eating habits of the family followed over generations, with minor adjustments wherever necessary to ensure a better balance of nutritional intake.

4. Keep away from alcoholic drinks and tobacco

It is quite obvious for any health-conscious person.

5. Sleep well

For a vast majority of people, at least 7 hours of sleep per day is essential. This requirement may vary by +/- 1 hour from person to person. Children need a couple of more hours of sleep per day. Should there be a shortfall in it, a healthy practice is to compensate for the shortfall in sleep by a "power nap" in the day time (if you can spare time) or by going to bed early on the next night.

6. Exercise regularly and moderately

Researchers have found that walking is the BEST form of exercise for all ages at all times. You can do moderate stretching exercises for about 15 minutes in the morning and about 30 to 45 minutes of walking in the evening. During the rest of the day, do not miss any opportunity to climb staircases. Where you have to walk up to two to 3 floors, always try to avoid using the Lift and grab the benefit of natural and unscheduled exercise by walking up the stairs.

Doing yoga (yoga asanas) is also very effective in giving strength to body and mind which has become very prevalent across the globe nowadays.

7. Avoid stresses and tension

If only your job, position, and work environment are conducive, you can try to pace your work according to YOUR convenience; By avoiding committing to unrealistic targets, excessively tight delivery schedules, and on tasks beyond your capacity, avoid unnecessary stresses and tensions. I firmly believe that ambition is anathema to healthy physical and mental well-being.

8. Be moderate in enjoying sensual pleasures

The ancient wisdom states that moderation is the key to happiness- whether it is satiating the palate, listening to music, watching TV, or indulgence in sex. If one moves from moderation to abstinence, he grows in spirituality and becomes worthy of enjoying the divine bliss at the appropriate time.

9. Do meditation

A disciplined way of life helps one to practice meditation and meditation consequently helps one to stay fit physically and mentally.

10. Have faith in the higher power

A firm faith in God with the right philosophical outlook helps one to discern what is within your control and what is beyond it; Put your best effort on what is within your control, but accept whatever God gives you as the fruit of your labor. If you are mostly able to accept with peace the happenings which are beyond your control, you will find that your physical health too improves as a consequence of mental peace.

These 10 tips will be of help to anyone who loves to stay fit and enjoy the consequences of it.

-=()=-

CHAPTER TWENTY-SEVEN

The Ideal Age Gap Between Man & Woman for Marriage

Is there a sound reason behind the traditional practice of women marrying older men? If so, how much older should the men be?

That's the crucial question. If a woman marries a man that is 7-10 years older than her, is she really marrying an "old(er) man?" Many women today seem to nurture such a viewpoint. Getting married to a man that is almost the same age (just two or three years older or even younger by one or two years) seems to be acceptable for today's woman. The question is whether such a trend and preference of present day women is in any way beneficial for her married life or not.

What does Hindu Shastras/ Smritis say on this subject? Are they relevant today?

Whatever Manu Smriti/ Parashara Smriti state on this subject has been totally irrelevant in the present day for the Hindus (and also by law too). The smritis say that a woman should be married off before her 12 th year i.e. before attaining puberty. They recommend an age gap of 12 to 20 years between husband and wife! Naturally, it is obvious that there is no question of even discussing the possibility of an older woman marrying a younger man!

Hence we can say that sastras do not offer any relevant help on this subject. We have to naturally rely on healthy practices that have been existing in society for long and go by their merits.

4-8 Years Is the Ideal Age Gap

Personally, I believe very strongly that an age difference of about 4 to 8 years between the woman and man (the man should be older, of course) is really conducive for a good marital bond, and it works very well in the majority of the cases that I have seen (of course taking all other favorable aspects of marriage between the man and woman).

Why It's Better for Women to Marry Older Men

1. Women Mature Faster Than Men

There are two elements of compatibility in a marital relationship: Physical maturity and mental maturity.

Women attain physical and mental maturity at a much younger age than men. A girl of three years has more advanced linguistic and oral communication skills than a boy of the same age and a girl's dependence on her mother at that age is far less than that of a boy. Furthermore, girls attend preschool with more ease, self-confidence, and willingness than boys.

A girl reaches puberty between the ages of 12 to 14 whereas a boy reaches it between 14 and 17. A girl's instincts about the opposite sex are much more developed as a teenager in comparison with boys.

At 21 years, a woman generally has well developed instincts to observe the world and people around her and frame judgments; she has fairly developed a sense of responsibility for her own life and those dependent herself and has firmed up clear ideas about her needs, wants, goals, and ambitions.

2. Men Aren't Ready for Marriage Until Later

On the other hand, a 21-yr-old man is far more boyish and carefree, taking things lightly and afraid of commitments and responsibility. An unbridled life as a bachelor is far more attractive to a man at that age than one of the commitment, responsibility and restrictions in a marital relationship.

Around the age of 26, men achieve the level of mental maturity required for a disciplined family life, which comes from the realization that the love and affection of a caring wife is far more valuable than a physical outlet for lust.

Thus, when a woman marries a man four to eight years older than her, they both have similar mental maturity levels and are in a better position to adjust to each other.

3. Women Respect Older Husbands More

All said and done, a basic psychological fact about men that cannot be wished away is his sense of superiority over the opposite sex. A man, deservedly or undeservedly, expects his wife to treat him as more than an equal partner. As such, he welcomes signs of respect.

Where there is a sizable age difference, the woman tends to show the man more respect. This psychological nuance helps in a significant way to bring harmony in the relationship.

4. Biology Favors Women Marrying Older Men

From a physical maturity point of view, an age difference augurs well in the long run. The best time for a woman to become a mother is before she turns 35, and her active interest in sex gradually wanes subsequently. She will reach menopause somewhere between 45 and 50. After menopause, women practically lose interest in sex.

On the other hand, a man's sexually virile age may extend even up to 60 years of age. At around 40, men tend to get a revived vigor in sexual cravings and a co-operative and willing partner at home helps prevent them from going astray.

5. Looks Matter as Decades Go By

Furthermore, having an attractive and young-looking wife is more important for men. For women, on the other hand, the man's love is more important than his looks. Normally, a 40-yr-old man would look quite youthful in comparison with his wife if she were of the same age.

Perhaps this is one of the main reasons why previous generations preferred a wider age gap between men and women in marriages.

About Men Marrying Older Women

I am biased totally against such an option. No separate arguments are needed as the logic behind the advantage of men marrying younger women was discussed earlier in this article.

There are many things in the present-day state of affairs, mentalities, values, and preferences that contradict time-tested practices and cultural guidelines. It is quite natural that the institution of marriage is getting a beating and many live without a happy conjugal relationship in the present generation.

Larger Age Gaps and Marriage Traditions

Marriages With Age Gaps of 10-12 Years Face Difficulties

If the age gap is much wider than 4-8 years, it is possible that the marriage will go sour in the long run. There are a few reasons why a woman might marry a man 12-15 years older than her.

It could be because of coercion or compulsion (by elders, through the husband's influence of power or intimidation, or because of the woman's economic insecurity). It could be because of illogical infatuation or psychological complexity. It could be a woman's calculated move to woo an older man for financial reasons. It could be to gain celebrity status through the back-door for a woman to marry an aged/ very elder male celebrity .

Unless there is a genuine bond of love and affection between the couple that can overcome the limitations of the sexual relationship in the long run, if the age gap is too wide there is always the danger of the marital bond breaking up with painful scars left behind.

Traditions of Marriage Are Changing

I write from India and many of my views are basically Indian. As the institution of marriage is still strong and respected in India, I am convinced that this system makes sense.

In India, even in my generation (I am 65+), it is rare to see women marrying men 10-12 years older than them as that practice has been virtually discontinued. In the generation prior to mine, there were a few cases here and there.

However, in at least one case, I knew a couple of my earlier generation with a 12-year age gap between them. They got married when the girl was just 14 and had no ideas of her own. In that generation, girls simply accepted their husbands like creepers winding around the trees. Perhaps that acceptance without questioning brought in a beautiful bonding between them.

The only problem their marriage faced was that the husband passed away when he was about 70 and his wife, aged 58, had a very long widowhood to be spent without her closest companion. She is quite fine now, living alone, but the lack of companionship at this old age does show in her emotional life.

Will the present day girl mold her life totally around such a "senior" husband unquestioningly? Will their life be free of a generation gap? Will the woman or man take it lightly if someone asks the girl "Is he your father?" It is very unlikely. In my opinion, a girl marrying a man who is ten years older or more is not a good proposition for the current times.

To conclude: Woman marrying a man 4 to 8 years older seems best.

Based on the various arguments that I have put above, it is my conclusion that there is a very fair scope for a successful marriage in the long run, if a woman marries a man 4 to 8 years older than her.

-=()=-

CHAPTER TWENTY-EIGHT

How to enjoy honeymoon bliss for ever

After marriage, the honeymoon stage involves couples remaining together most of the time, going sightseeing and engaging in love making as frequently as possible. Honeymoon stage is the period where romance peaks and starts fading and the intimacy brings into much closer focus the partner's "real nature" more and more.

How far the couple is able to digest the fading away of "over-bloated" romanticism and accept each other's "real nature" forms the backbone of enjoying marital bliss even after the honeymoon stage.

Accepting the other person's true nature involves lots of give and take; a high degree of predominance of love over lust; a willingness to dilute some of your rigid likes and dislikes that you were fiercely clutching hitherto; a fair degree of taming of your egotism; a capacity to be receptive to criticism and a good sense of humor to laugh at your own idiosyncrasies. Above all it requires a firm commitment to the sanctity of the institution of marriage.

By the time the honeymoon ends, the couple becomes too familiar to each other. This familiarity factor brings in lots of relaxation in one's cultivated good habits and manners subsequently; you start taking your partner for granted and you remove some of your masks. It is quite natural. But throwing them away totally into dustbins is rather uncalled for. Accepting that the honeymoon period was blissful for the couple, carrying through some of your cultivated habits and manners during the honeymoon even after honeymoon albeit in a diluted way can help sustain the marital bliss.

Here are some of them:

What Women Should Do to Prolong Marital Bliss Beyond Honeymoon

During your honeymoon, of course, you spoke a lot, but you heard him a lot too. You were all ears to hear his fond memories, his achievements on the job and so on. Continue this to a fair degree post honeymoon.

You were too glad to please him always during your honeymoon; you derived pleasure in pleasing him. Because he was not so far too intimately familiar to you, you were somewhat modest and wanted to show some respect to him for his age, masculinity, knowledge - whatever. Men secretly enjoy this modesty of yours and the respect they get from partners; carry a fair degree of it after the honeymoon too.

You were willing to accept changes in your dress code and taste, your social behavior (particularly with other men-folk, with his relatives) etc. Continue with these adjustments in the long term interest.

What men Should Do to Prolong Marital Bliss Beyond Honeymoon

You know (or you should know, if you so far didn't know) that for woman, romance does not mean sex alone. There is romance in holding hands, being together, talking sweet nothings, listening to others, playfulness, spending quality time together, extending a helping hand to her at her chores etc. The more you do them after the honeymoon stage, the more you are poised for a blissful marital life.

Take care of your personal hygiene, grooming and manners. Were you not extremely careful with these things during your honeymoon? Continue with a more-than-a-fair share of them afterward too.

Did not television, news channels and channel-surfing take the last priority for you in the late evenings during your honeymoon? Were you not too willing to hear her speak, make comments in between and make it obvious that you were listening to her in all seriousness? Why not continue to nurture this habit to a good degree after marriage?

You showed respect to her relatives, behaved decently with women of opposite sex, curtailed you ogling tendencies etc immediately after your marriage. These are not habits to be thrown away into a dustbin.

Your partner's moods, physical discomfiture, occasional disinclination towards love-making etc are to be respected; never treat your partner as an object of desire to satiate your selfish animal instincts. This is one characteristic that can sustain a good marital relationship for long.

Marriage is a commitment of mutual loyalty. Any slackening of this loyalty will rob you of marital bliss and also mental peace in the long run.

Here are some more points for both husbands and wives to ponder about and adopt, for enjoying marital bliss on a continuing basis even after the honeymoon stage:

The familiarity factor reduces the sexual urge over a period of time following honeymoon period. But habits die hard. You do not really have to engage in sex on a daily basis just because you have been doing so till recently. Change the focus from quantity to quality. Be creative in experimenting new ways of being intimate and never allow the fun element to get replaced by a duty-bound, variety-less mechanical act. When each partner's intent is focused on satisfying the other first rather than self gratification first, the fundamentals of a blissful family life are laid strong.

Cultivate closest friendliness with your spouse. This advice may surprise many, but the reality in life of most married couples seems to be that a sense of friendship does not exist in adequate measure between couples. Many men and women seem to think that a friend to confide your innermost feelings and thoughts and to seek counsel when mentally troubled should be outside the marital bond! Far from true. A corollary to this advice is that post marriage, you should learn to keep your erstwhile bosom friends at an arms distance, and never allow them to meddle in your privacy, if they had such an access in the past.

Make sure to the best of your ability by discussing, sharing and planning, to get your first child at a period of your willful choice. Of course quite a lot depends on the will of a supreme force in begetting a child; but human effort and planning are not totally out of place. At least a one year period of intimacy and closeness between a husband and wife will be very beneficial for building a blissful married life in the long run, before the child's arrival is planned. If only the arrival of a child becomes an eagerly anticipated incident rather than an accidental happening, marital harmony will definitely get a boost.

A man marries a woman whereas a woman marries a family. A lot depends on the woman in ensuring a harmonious family life; let not possessiveness in the garb of love interfere in the erstwhile relations of the husband's and wife's families. A happily co-existing family circle is extremely essential for a blissful family life and this can only be ensured by the spreading of love and not by the narrow possessiveness of love.

The seeds of a blissful married life are more or less sown at the time of honeymoon. Some seeds may grow to a sapling without much nurturing, but mostly one has to take care to water the soil, protect the seed from getting eaten away by ants and so on before it grows into a sapling. Likewise a blissful relation post honeymoon requires good nurturing by the couple.

-=()=-

CHAPTER TWENTY-NINE

What is the ideal age gap between two children

Do you know that the nature itself has paved the way for adequate age gap between two children by relating breastfeeding of the newborn baby to the onset of next ovulation?

It is a real natural wonder that nature has designed that the woman should breastfeed her child and the more regularly she does it, the more the onset of next ovulation gets delayed. Statistics show that for regularly breastfeeding women, the menstrual cycle restarts in about 20 weeks after delivery.

Unfortunately, many present day mothers do not seem to breastfeed their children all that regularly. So, in reality, the time gap between two children is influenced by a plethora of factors concerned with the couple. Predominant among them could be just accidental!

Accidental

Let us face it. Many times, the couple may want to adequately space the time between two children; but somewhere down the line, a slackening of guards, or a missed calculation about the safe periods of unprotected intercourse in the "rhythm cycle" may cause an unplanned pregnancy at much earlier period; The revelation about having conceived unexpectedly might somewhat depress the couple; however, many affectionate ones, who have tasted the bliss of having a cute lovable little darling for once, accept it gracefully as God's scheme of things. There are of course couples who opt for an abortion with a heavy feeling of guilt.

The economic factor

Having a child and nurturing it has quite a lot of cost implications. The cost of prenatal care, delivery, postnatal care, pediatric health care, cost of child food, medical treatments, dress and accessories - all have the potential to eat away a large chunk of income. The parents should make sure that they are adequately well off to take care of these fresh expenses before planning the next child.

The love and joy factor

Some parents love their current child so much that they find it too difficult even to think of sharing that love with another child. Up to an age of 3, the little child radiates so much joy and divinity. As the child grows up and starts to go to school, it gradually develops "human qualities" - stubbornness, throwing up tantrums, irritability, sneakiness, falsehood etc . Now the parents start missing the hitherto attractive divinity in the child and it is at that point of time they think of having another baby to bring back the "paradise lost"!

The mother's health factor

Not all mothers remain healthy after a child-birth. If the delivery was done using a Cesarean section, the woman's health does get affected to a perceptible extent. Doctors normally advise a minimum gap of 1 year before getting pregnant again; conventional wisdom says that it is better to give a longer gap to ensure that the scars of the section get adequately rebuilt and hence any longer gap (more than 1 year) is preferable. There is always the risk of having the next delivery too by cesarean section, which adds further complication to the woman's long term health.

The mother's age factor

There are different and contradicting medical view-points about the safe upper age limit for a woman to bear a child; Ignoring extreme cases, we could say that an age below 35 years would be a generally safe and agreeable limit from the points of view of the mother's health and the long term parenting responsibilities.

Where the couple is keen to have more than one child and assuming that the woman gave birth to her first child only at an advanced age of about 33, it may not be out of place in this case for the woman to become pregnant again quickly, leaving a time gap of just 2 years between the children. In such specific cases, the disadvantages of bearing children at a more advanced age far outweigh the disadvantages of having babies at a much shorter gap.

The child's health factor

Where the existing child has some congenital health problems or any frequently occurring ailments, it naturally demands lots of continuing care from the mother and until the time the condition of the child improves considerably, the parents can not obviously think of another child.

The sibling rivalry factor

I have personally seen that where the age gap between two children is too short (1.5 to 3 years), the elder child develops a marked sibling rivalry towards the younger one. Though a thread of affection will always be present between the children undoubtedly, the rivalry would tend to continue albeit very subtly even when they grow up.

It is my personal observation that when the age gap between children is slightly more (above 4 up to 5 years), the elder one starts yearning for the company of a little brother or a sister, and is able to welcome the new child with more affection and less of rivalry.

Assuming that all factors are favorably placed, I would personally recommend a gap of four to five years as the ideal gap between two children.

CHAPTER THIRTY

How to learn successful marriage tips from India

Globally, marital discords and divorces continue to be on the rise and there have always been questions whether there could be a better alternative to a man-woman relationship other than a formal marriage. However no human society has ever found a better alternative to the institution of marriage.

It is obvious that there is nothing fundamentally wrong in the arrangement of marriage, but it is only the attitude of people towards the time-tested bondage that has created problems for the institution.

In countries like India, unlike the western society, marriages continue to hold the traditional reverence and despite the onslaught of globalization and the resulting cross currents of cultural invasions, marriages are far more successful in India and divorce rates are far fewer than in any other developed country.

We can definitely take some clues from Indian culture on how to ensure a lasting marital relationship. Be forewarned that some of the ideas discussed here may look archaic and unpalatable to feminists in particular.

The woman's primary role as a mother and a homemaker

Indian culture has had its ups and downs in its vast history on the status of a woman (right from child marriage, sati, denial of education etc, to the present level of giving equal opportunities to women in education, employment, national governance, police and even in armed forces). But, even today, in the mindsets of people including a vast majority of educated and career oriented women, the woman's primary and most respected role is motherhood and her predominant role in society is as a protector and nurturer of the household and family relationships.

Parents, grandparents, in-laws, uncles, aunts, cousins, nephews and nieces -- the Indian culture revolves around relationships rather than friendships. A woman acts as the binding force between all the individuals related to the family. So, in India, it is said that when a man marries, he just marries a woman, whereas a woman marries a family.

A woman, even if she is looked at as a sex object before marriage, transforms to a venerable mother once she gets married and bears a child. Even in today's transformed culture of nucleus families where selfishness is gradually becoming a virtue, Indian society gives the greatest respect to a married woman who never breaks families and who ensures cordial relationships with all her in-laws and other relatives.

When it comes to ensuring cordiality of relationship and welfare of children, lots of Indian women still opt to become stay-at-home moms, giving top-most priority to home rather than their careers.

Getting married at the most appropriate age

Even though men and women attain majority at the age of 18, in well educated and cultured families in India, the woman gets married above 20 years and the man above 25 years. It is at this age that both men and women understand the institution of marriage better and are mature enough to face the challenges of running a family.

Ensuring adequate age difference between husband and wife

As most of the marriages in India are still arranged marriages, parents generally look for an age difference of 3 to 6 years, the boy obviously being older. In some stray cases, age differences of even 8 to 10 years too are accepted. There is a very sound logic in this preference.

A girl attains puberty at about 12 to 14 years whereas a boy attains it at 14 to 17 years of age. There is a proportionate difference in their mental maturities too. Qualities like judging people, sense of responsibility towards one's own life and that of those dependent on oneself, firming up clear ideas about one's needs, wants, ambitions etc are reasonably well developed in a woman at about 21 years.

On the other hand, a man of equal age is far more boyish, carefree and is afraid of getting into commitments and taking up responsibility. An unbridled life of freedom looks to be far more attractive to a man at that age. A man gets to grasp the importance and the responsibilities of a disciplined married life mostly above the age of 26.

Thus when a woman of 21 marries a man 4 to 5 years elder to her, the mental maturity level between them fairly matches and they will be in a better position to adjust with each other.

Fundamentally, a man, deservedly or undeservedly expects his wife to treat him as more than an equal partner. When a decent age difference exists, the woman tends to show him more respect than if he were to be of equal age to her. This psychological nuance helps in a significant way in bringing cordiality in a relationship.

A woman attains menopause anywhere between her 45th to 50th age. After menopause, women drastically lose interest in sex. On the other hand, a man's sexually virile age may extend even up to his 60 years of age. Man at around 40th of age tends to get a revived vigor in sexual cravings and a co-operative, young and a willing partner at home helps in preventing him from going astray.

Ensuring cultural compatibility

Basic human tendency is to feel comfortable and be at ease with people of their own religion, language, clan, color, sect/ sub-sect, food habits, cultural practices etc. In India, this comes through the caste system. Most parents insist on getting their children married within their castes or with sub-sects compatible with each other.

In India, religion plays a very powerful role in everyday life. Love marriages, cutting across religious, cultural and caste barriers do not mostly succeed in India. Even highly educated people who consider themselves modern, have their sentiments deeply attached to such things, even though they may deny it outwardly.

Since family relationship is a predominant factor in social relationships, arranged marriages, with a large parental influence and with due concurrence with the man and woman to be wedded, are highly successful in India when compared to love marriages where families have been sidelined.

Ensuring chastity of the man and woman

In Indian culture, chastity of man and woman before marriage is considered very important and sacred. Even in today's highly loosened morality aided and abetted by the onslaught of globalization and westernization, a vast majority of marriages in India do take place between chaste men and women. And that's one of the reasons why Indian culture and family structure remains intact across centuries.

Having faith in the compatibility of horoscopes

In many Indian social segments, marriages are arranged after checking the compatibility of the horoscopes of the man and woman under wedlock. There is an increased resistance from the younger generation to this practice.

Marital failures do happen, whether arranged marriages or love marriages. But since a vast majority of arranged marriages, done by checking the compatibility of horoscopes, is able to remain intact, despite skirmishes and petty fights between husbands and wives, there is definitely scope in believing that this age-old practice has some validity.

Developing lifelong commitment to marriage

In India, marriage is considered a sacred relationship, meant for lifelong togetherness. No marriage is ever experimented with an idea like "if something does not work out, we shall get separated without any qualms and look for an alternative relationship".

Again, in line with global trends in India too, utter selfishness, excessive egotism and high degree of impatience have started playing havoc in several marriages. But if you consider a vast majority again, the commitment to the sanctity of marriage is very strong.

Giving top most priority to the well-being of the children

Despite the burgeoning population, India's love for children is very strong. The arrival of a baby in the family is always a celebration that brings disgruntled people together. A baby cures several wounds in marital disharmony. Parents not seeing eye to eye with each other continue to live together in marital bond, purely for the sake of happiness and well being of the children. And wonderfully, this singular decision brings back a fresh lease of life to the dying marital relationship in many cases.

Indian society, despite the presence of a large number of well educated and independent-thinking women in the society, still does not treat a divorcee too gently. A divorced woman, rightly or wrongly, is somehow looked down upon as someone who has not learned the art of adjustment, and give-and-take so essential in marriage. A divorcee getting re-married is still an uphill task, though changes are coming in this aspect gradually in Indian society.

To conclude...

The cultural glory of a country or a society is very strongly linked to the stability of marriages and relationships. A stable marriage ensures a cultured upbringing of children; Stable marriage is an indicator of peace, tolerance, harmony, unselfishness and stability in the society. Indians may still be economically backward when compared to people in western countries but, Indian culture has got certain very precious and noble things to showcase to the outer world. The Indian marriage institution is one of them.

CHAPTER THIRTY-ONE

How to make marriage really last for a lifetime

A good marriage is like a delicacy. The recipe should be complete, all the ingredients must be in the right proportions, the cooking should be done on the fire over the stipulated time and served neatly and sumptuously when hungry. A marriage can last forever, just like the lingering taste of a well prepared delicacy, provided all the aspects and ingredients of marriage are perfect.

When something slightly goes amiss in cooking, an expert chef knows how to adjust and manipulate contents to ensure that the end product is ensured to be of acceptable quality. In a similar way, partners in marriage should also know the knack of adjusting for the sake of ensuring long lasting relationships in marriage.

What are the successful ingredients of a marriage that can last forever?

Trust in the sanctity of the institution of marriage

Marriage is just not for ensuring an outlet for the natural sexual urges for human body alone; it is a socially acceptable and time-tested practice followed across all human societies for the canalization of sexual energy in a respectable way to ensure continuation of progeny. In this process, the trust and commitment of the couple to each other is basic. The aim of marriage is a life-long togetherness for mutual care, support and for bringing up children as worthy citizens of the future.

For these to be ensured, a basic, almost "religious" trust in the institution of marriage is of paramount importance. Any marriage proposal based on fleeting attraction of the opposite sexes, mostly glorified as love for the sake of legitimacy, without a sense of commitment for long term relationship can never ensure longevity of marriage.

Of course, things can go awry in a marital relationship. Failures of marriage may be seen as the only practical reality of life all around. But that should not be a cause for entering into a marital relationship without the basic trust in the sanctity of marriage. You cannot make prayers without faith in God.

Mutual respect and affection

Love is a word, which is too emotional, many times very artificially interpreted, frequently confused with love-making and many times having too short a life span in marriage. For a marriage to last forever, the transient love should mature into mutual affection with an element of respect for each other. The respect need not be interpreted like the type of respect children of previous generations were expected to hold on their parents.

It is respect combined with intimacy; giving credit to the other person what is rightfully due; giving the independent breathing space; showing respect to the other's relatives and friends; giving respect to the other's principles, values and beliefs; having trust in each other.

Need for a good foundation

Love and love-making enliven marriage in early stages and undoubtedly they are essential ingredients in the formative stages of marriage. However, in a long lasting marriage, what is basic staple food in the beginning turns to a "side dish" over time! This should be natural. Satiating hunger of the flesh should not be the long lasting role of love and sex in marriage.

Being self-centered: Yes. Being selfish: No

There is a thick veil of difference between being self-centered and being selfish. Many people do not grasp the difference between the two.

Every individual has physical, emotional and intellectual needs - income/ financial freedom, creature comforts, love, care, respect, social status etc. If people go behind acquiring these needs with least concern about the trouble and discomfort caused to others in the process, they are selfish. On the other hand, as long as one goes in pursuit of acquiring these needs without intentionally and arrogantly causing trouble and inconvenience to the spouse in a marital relationship, they are self-centered needs.

When the spouse is willing to adjust, accommodate and even sacrifice to some extent to the self-centered needs of the partner, the marriage can last forever but certainly not under selfish machinations of one over the other partner.

Absence of egotism

Strange though it may be, it is not uncommon to see people, who are basically far less egoistic with friends and relatives, behaving egotistically with their spouses! Some women will talk freely about many personal matters with friends, cut jokes, allow others close to them to make fun of them but they will not be found to be so free and jovial with their husbands. Some husbands too behave in a similar way. Some husbands will not tolerate their wives cutting jokes about their idiosyncrasies in public.

Some wives will flare up if their husband cracks any jokes about their culinary skills amidst his relatives. Some will not tolerate even slight criticism about their looks or habits by their spouses. The husband and wife may have been living together for several years but you won't find the casualness of a good friendship between them.

Lack of egotism in the relationship between husband and wife is of prime importance in ensuring a lasting relationship with a bond that will be visible to others. With such a quality built in the psyche, forgiving and forgetting comes naturally. A bitter fight of today can be laughed off across the dining table the very next day, without leaving a taste of bitterness behind.

Accept the difference between a man and woman

Another wrong concept that breaks the basics of marriage is the idea of equality between man and woman in marriage. Man and woman are not equal. They join in a relationship to complement each other - not to become equal to each other. A woman's power lies in her capacity to love, give, share and care. A man's power lies in being the breadwinner, the protector and the leader. Man dominates by physical means and a woman balances and tames him by her emotional strength.

Where this basic difference is clearly understood, the marriage can last forever.

=-

CHAPTER THIRTY-TWO

How to understand men in a marital relationship

Men, unlike women, are far easier to understand. Most men are very eager to understand women, but they are not really shrewd enough for the task since women are not open enough to be understood easily! On the other hand, women are quite shrewd to understand men who are far less complicated a creation of God, provided women are eager enough to observe and learn!

What do women basically want from men? Security, loyalty, love, understanding and emotional support. To get some or all these from men, women have got to make certain sacrifices in life and a good understanding of men can help women a lot in this respect.

A word of caution: Some of the ideas discussed in this article may be quite unpalatable to feminists. Not all men will fit into the stereotypes discussed here.

Man wants some degree of respect from his woman

Whether he deserves it or not, whether he can reciprocate it or not, man wants his woman to show some degree of respect to him. This expectation may come in several forms:

- Giving him the pleasure of delivering the last word in an argument or in decision making

- Not shouting at him back over and above his voice in an argument
- Not rubbing him at the wrong side when he is in an irritable mood
- Not seriously criticizing him or complaining about him to his friends and dear ones (but making fun of his idiosyncrasies in a light hearted way without intentionally hurting him is okay)
- Not trying to dominate him in an authoritative or commanding voice or manners
- Not commanding or demanding his support or assistance in doing or sharing domestic chores as a matter of right.

Most men do not 'really' believe in 'equal partnership' in marital relationship

Even though they may eulogize such a relationship verbally, most men, heart of heart, believe in the dictum of the Orwellian Jungle – "some animals are more equal than others"! There are deep psychological reasons behind it. We shall come to them later in this article.

Whether he truly deserves one-upmanship or not, man thinks and believes that, whatever be the qualities that his woman may possess better than him – be it good looks, age, education, proficiency in fine arts, earnings or professional status, his status as "man" is one step above all these of a woman. He cannot easily digest any domination of his woman on the strength of any of these qualities. He may compromise and accept domination by the woman due to practical or selfish considerations in the short term, but the basic resistance will always be seething inside him, and it will show its ugly head one day or another.

A Man's mental maturity is mostly a shade less than that of a woman of same age

This is one of the reasons why a woman is generally advised to marry a man older than her. Women attain both physical and mental maturity at much younger age than men. A girl attains puberty at about 12 to 14 years where as a boy attains it at 14 to 17 years of age. A girl's instinct about the opposite sex is much more developed at the teen age in comparison with boys.

Seeing the world and observing people, sense of responsibility towards one's own life and that of those dependent on oneself, firming up of clear ideas about one's needs and wants, goals and ambitions etc are reasonably well developed in a woman at about 21 years; on the other hand, a man of comparable age is far more boyish, carefree, takes things too lightly and is afraid of getting into commitments and taking up responsibility. An unbridled, play-boy life looks to be far more attractive to a man at that age than one of commitment and responsibility of a marital relationship.

A level of mental maturity towards a disciplined family life and the realization that love and affection of a caring wife is far more valuable than a physical outlet for lust comes to a man somewhere above the age of twenty six or so.

Sexual urge in a man is much more strong and explicit than in women

And it remains over a much longer age.

The sexual urge and overt need of sexual gratification get subsided in a woman to an extent once she becomes a mother. After the age of 35, a woman's sexual urges get toned down and in her late forties the woman attains menopause which, on most women, drastically curbs her sexual needs.

That's not the case with men. Men sexual urges remain strong for quite long and their virility can extent even up to the age of 60. Men's sexual urges get excited through their visual faculty predominantly. That's why, man's inherent tendency to ogle at shapely women shamelessly remains in them, unmindful of their aging. The reason for most men viewing pornography irrespective of their age, maturity, marital status, objections from partners etc is primarily because of their getting sexual arousal through the visual medium.

To state crudely, this tendency of men is akin to a dog's "natural urge to urinate" at the sight of a lamp-post!

A woman is essentially designed to be a "mother" by nature; but a man has no such natural fatherly instincts

Emotionally and biologically, a woman reaches her "wholeness" only through motherhood. That's how God has created her. But that's not the case with men. Most women are natural mothers. Most men are not natural fathers. Fatherly love is something that a man cultivates, aided and inspired by the love of the mother and the attraction of Godliness in a child. No man can ever play the role of a mother to his children, whatever be the extent of his love.

A man loves to be loved like a mother by his wife

A man's bonding to his mother, by nature, is much stronger than a woman's bonding to her mother. A man, heart of heart, craves for the motherly tender care from his wife; he loves to have her attention, cuddling, her concern on his welfare, her cooking and filling his stomach with the foods of his taste and so on.

A man willingly submits to woman's domination only through love

As we have seen in point (1) above, a man cannot, by nature, tolerate an authoritatively dominating woman. But the same man willingly submits to his wife, provided she floors him by her love, affection, commitment and loyalty to him and her care of their family and children. Fortunately, God has given all these qualities to women, but some women who cannot digest this simple natural fact, tend to play the wrong cards and lose the game in their lives.

Men are far less expressive verbally, unlike women

Men believe that their feelings and love are to be better understood by their actions than words. Many men get exasperated by women's natural tendency to expect expression of love, even if it sounds too artificial, through the words of men.

Man's basic instincts always makes him believe that his role and responsibility is essentially outside the house

That's why he has lots of mental resistance to extend help in domestic chores to his wife; while on one hand he comfortably enjoys the monetary benefits of an employed wife bringing in money, he assiduously and selfishly tends to ignore the moral obligation to return favors to his wife by way of sharing her domestic chores.

Physical bruteness and polygamist tendencies in a man of today are highly subdued, but remain buried deep inside

On account of gradual evolution, education and cultural growth, men's animal-like aggressive instincts and polygamist tendencies have been highly toned down, but they remain very much deeply buried in most men's psyche.

It's a woman's tenderness, capacity to love him despite all his weaknesses and her inclination to lean on him for security, support and succor that makes the brute in the man to behave nicely with his woman. A man, heart of heart, thinks that he has compromised a lot from his basic instincts and that he deserves that much extra love, respect and one-upmanship in his relationship with the woman.

Many men believe that women are gifted better histrionic capabilities that men can not match on equal footing

Such men believe that if a woman can assault and hurt them with words, they have the right to use physical force to counter it and think there is nothing wrong in it. If a man is expected to digest a woman's verbal onslaught post-fight, he thinks a woman is expected to digest his physical assault and call it a truce.

Over and above all these, there are several other unique aspects of men that are normally discussed in many books of psychology and those points are not repeated here.

If a woman can understand all these fine psychological realities about a man, she gets the right key to handle her man the right way. Women of previous generations had a better grasp of this reality than the present generation and they were far more successful in walking over the knife edge of life than the women of the present generation, who expect, want and demand total equality. Families break on account of such misunderstandings and women continue to remain the most emotionally affected lot in the bargain.

-=()

CHAPTER THIRTY-THREE

Monogamy – Is it nature or nurtured?

It really appears that God has created men with some undue advantages and privileges over women. Perhaps on account of this advantageous position, the basic mental and physical tendency of a man is polygamous; on the other hand, due to the physical and mental nature of women, they tend to be more monogamous. Thus there lies a natural phenomenon that leads one to subscribe that monogamy in a woman is her "nature" and in a man it develops by "nurturing".

Motherhood and monogamy in woman

God seems to have created every woman with the intention of making her life wholesome essentially through her motherhood. This mother instinct is deeply etched in every female species, including the animal kingdom. Amidst human beings, even the life of a nymphomaniac undergoes a metamorphosis, both physiologically and emotionally, once she gives birth to a baby. The inexplicable bondage of love a woman develops with her baby and the desire to protect and nurture the child calls for an emotional attachment towards the man who was the cause of the arrival of the child.

In a woman, God seems to have made this emotional bondage with her man and her sense of loyalty associated with it very strong indeed. Added to this natural phenomenon, there exist the moral and ethical standards imposed by society on women. The society as a whole imposes (or expects) the morality of monogamy in a woman and it cannot simply be brushed aside accusing that it is males' scheme of things to subjugate women this way. No woman possessing basic moral values ever respects a woman who practices polygamy. It is not again because of traditional moral conditioning, but because, deep within her psyche every woman seems to feel comfortable and peaceful with having just one man as the father of her children.

It is true that in the present day scheme of things where marital discords and divorces have become too common, a woman may bear the children of more than one father one marriage after another (what is now called serial monogamy) , but definitely the society would not easily accept a woman having more than one sexual partner simultaneously.

Thus along with motherhood, God appears to have given a woman a far deeper sense of responsibility towards her children and the need to ensure their respectability in the society; that respectability can be ensured by her only by declaring boldly, without any sense of guilt, who their singular father is.

A woman's psyche, by nature, is haunted by a high degree of guilt and consequent emotional turmoil, if she were to become polygamous by her adventurism, omissions or commissions.

A man can sow seeds everywhere

Contrary to all the above, think of a man's physical and emotional constitution. Man's life is NOT built physically and mentally around fatherhood. When a woman produces just one egg in her womb per month that has the potential to become a child, a man produces billions and billions of sperms at every ejaculation which he is capable of releasing every day. A man, like a tree or a plant produces far in excess of seeds that can create a new life. Why is it so? It leads us to believe that it is purely God's scheme of things that it be so.

This excess and natural production of seeds tempt a man to sow them at wider and newer fields and he is not haunted by any emotional sense of guilt as strongly as women are. That's why there is lot of scope to conclude that God has not created men to be monogamous strictly;He has given him the freedom to play as he likes and face the physical and emotional consequences of practicing such an unbridled freedom, or to restrain himself by accepting moral and spiritual responsibility towards a single woman.

Enforcing monogamy through womanly love and care

God has also given, in a very poetic way, some strong capabilities to women to keep her man bonded and hooked to her without going astray. Yes. It is the power of a woman's overpowering love, possessiveness and the physical bondage she weaves around a man. It is this beautiful characteristic of woman that attracts and binds a man to one woman. A woman's way of showing love to her man, the way she goes about satisfying his needs and nurturing him, the way she displays extraordinary motherly characteristics to their children and the extent of sacrifice a women does to do her divinely role of playing the unselfish motherhood — all these create an awe in a man on his wife.

Loving, nurturing, caring, accepting man's dominance, accepting a man's many idiosyncrasies and still tolerating and supporting him — all these things are done by women just as a barter deal to ensure men of predominantly polygamous tendencies to remain monogamous. Thus a woman plays her role naturally to nurture monogamous tendencies in a man.

An essentially polygamous man can be tamed and turned monogamous only through the unique strengths, well founded on femininity, as endowed to a woman by God. When women forget to grasp this simple fact, they end up fighting for equality and entangle themselves into more and more emotional turmoil.

If a man, despite his natural and inborn tendency, opts to live monogamous, he is definitely elevating himself spiritually. By nurturing this quality, he may lose some thrills and fun in life, but he gains love, physical well being, mental peace and tranquility in the bargain. On the contrary, if a woman tends to become polygamous, she is going against her basic monogamous nature and thus tend to acquire lowly animal qualities. As women are more of emotional creatures than men, a fallen woman suffers a lot more emotionally than a fallen man.

Such of those women who want equality with men in all respects — women who want to shun their traditional role and monogamous nature and compete with men in all spheres including the domain of loosened moralities, are woefully ignorant of this elementary fact, and the price they pay for it in their physical and mental plane is really too stiff.

The suffering of a family or a society is much more when a woman goes astray, than when a man goes astray. This is not an area where women should try for equality with men. If they do, not only do they bring themselves to ruin, but also cause severe damage to the balance of the society at large.

Monogamy & Polygamy – Potent Lessons from Indian Mythology

Lord Rama, the most adored male Monogamist

In the grand Hindu Epic Ramayana, King Rama practiced monogamy as a matter of great virtue, despite the fact that it was quite a common norm those days that Kings had multiple wives. Rama's father Dasaratha had three queens and other 60 concubines in his palace and Lord Rama never took it as an example to follow for his personal life. With such great virtue, Rama is being adored as the ideal husband, despite the fact that he got himself separated from his dear wife Sita and sent her to forest in order to uphold his adherence to dharma as a ruler.

Draupadi, the much condemned woman polygamist

On the contrary, in the other grand Hindu epic Mahabharata, the 5 pandavas, who were considered sticklers to dharma, got infatuated by the overpowering beauty of Draupadi; they opted to marry her as a common wife of all the five, despite the fact that it was only Arjuna who won her by his archery skills at the swayamvara of Draupadi. There are explanations and justifications given in this mythology for this deviant act, but the fact remains that Draupadi accepted this proposition without protest; it was quite a blasphemous act, even considering the fact that the morality of the ruling class was at its lowest ebb during Mahabharata period.

This act against the social norm practiced by Draupadi and Pandavas can be taken as one of the covert causes of the many hardships faced by the Pandavas in their lives. The total lack of empathy towards their cause by the Kauravas and the utter disrespect meted out to them by kauravas becomes very obvious when Pandavas lost everything to Kauravas while playing the dice game. Draupadi was singled out and utterly humiliated by Karna as he was openly laughing at Draupadi, calling her a whore that married 5 men and she could very well come and sit on his lap too.

It should be noted that though Pandavas won the war, none of their children given birth by Draupadi was alive to rule the kingdom later.

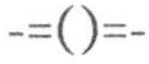

CHAPTER THIRTY-FOUR

Dos and Don'ts of Personal Finance

Surprisingly, some of the fundamental dos and don'ts in personal finance are really never new. Those were the principles your grandfathers and great grandfathers were practicing in their ages. The only difference was that there was not so much of consumerism those days; there were not so many truly-unnecessary-but-highly-ensnaring products and gadgets in the market and the curse of the credit card culture was non-existent.

Unfortunately, for the present day spendthrifts who want instant gratification through un-owned money , those age-old fundamentals of sound personal finance practices may sound bland and boring. But only experience will tell you that olden wisdom is always aimed at giving long lasting peace than enjoying short-spanned thrills in life.

Live within your means

It simply means: let your regular expenses be well within your regular income. It amounts to saying that let your desires, needs and ambitions be restricted in proportion to your income; let your lifestyle be in tune with your current earnings and not in comparison with your neighbor, colleague or a peer.

Save a percentage of your income

There is a saying: Let your first expenditure be a saving. While we go about happily with undisciplined spending, we normally find it difficult to do disciplined saving. Saving should become a commitment. The culture of saving should be nurtured in our blood stream.

How much to save? A general guideline is 10% of your income, at the least; The more, the better.

Never enjoy luxury on borrowed money

The toughest rule is never to borrow money, which perhaps might not have been practical for the vast majority even in those days. The relaxed rule is to borrow money only for buying long term assets (like a house).

A further relaxed rule is to borrow money for capital intensive luxuries (like buying a car). But the age old wisdom restricts borrowing to cover only that much of money which you can't pump in from your savings. The idea is that your debts should be minimal and well within your capacity to repay without much sweat. It goes without saying that the choice and model of the vehicle you buy on loans should be what you can afford to repay comfortably and not what is prestigious to own.

Invest on assets that appreciate faster or that have higher security value

An investment on a piece of land has more scope of appreciation and has higher security value than company shares. Investment in gold may not have faster appreciation but has a sound security value.

Extending this principle to today's context, your great grandfather would not approve of investing money in an apartment; he would rather prefer to buy an independent house on a plot of land, even if it is quite farther away in a suburb with much reduced plinth area.

Distribute investments more in low-risk low-return avenues and less on high-risk, high-return avenues

The olden wisdom was always more in favor of security, stability and less on speculation and risk. Long term, slow growth was given a lot more weightage over short-term high growth.

Where income is limited, do not own what you can hire

Be it a house or a car - unless you can safely repay the money you borrow without cutting too many corners on the luxuries that you are comfortably enjoying today within your current means, it is not advisable to go for ownership.

Write your personal accounts; avoid unplanned, impulsive purchases

Every house-holder is supposed to write their daily expenditure accounts; Budgeting is a mandatory discipline. Impulsive and unplanned purchases are to be meticulously avoided.

We can definitely "borrow " such a few good things from the past generation about managing our personal finance. Olden values were built on one watchword - integrity. Your honesty and integrity get subjected to maximum trials and tribulations if you borrow beyond your means. Becoming bankrupt was tantamount to walking naked on the street in olden days. If only we can follow a few of these guidelines, we can be free from the burden of debts and can ever be indebted to our forefathers for their practical wisdom.

-=()=-

CHAPTER THIRTY-FIVE

Saving Tips – how to Save Money Fast

Stop spending money fast and consequently you will start saving money fast! Except for those born with thrift running in their blood, the tendency to spend money the moment one has cash in hand is a universal tendency. The more successful we are in curbing this tendency, the faster we can save money.

Here are some good tips for saving money fast:

Make saving as your first expenditure

Bring in a discipline to put a certain percentage of your monthly paycheck into a recurring deposit, immediately after receiving the paycheck. The best way to do it is to open a recurring deposit in your bank account and give standing instructions to your bankers to debit the specified amount from your account to the savings on the pay day.

Avoid unnecessary visits to shopping malls

A visit to a shopping mall will tempt you to buy unnecessary things that catch your eye in addition to essential things in your grocery list. Visiting a local shop to buy your goods is a better idea than visiting huge shopping malls. Better still, give your monthly, budgeted shopping list to your local shop and if the shop offers facilities for door delivery, utilize it. The idea is to discourage you from getting tempted at the dazzling display of unwanted goods at shops that tend to drain your wallet unnecessarily.

Buy on cash rather than on credit

Though this discipline is difficult to enforce in today's credit card culture, you can always make a genuine attempt to buy things only on cash. Since cash transactions are dwindling day by day, the other alternative is to use your debit card rather than credit card. It helps you in two ways: One, every time you spend your hard earned cash, you feel a pinch at your heart; two, you won't get the temptation to defer the payment to the credit card company when the bill comes and consequently spend heavily on interests.

Simplify life

Avoid frequent eating outs; keep away from parties; stop celebrating birthdays; never greet others with bouquets; reduce giving gifts to near and dear ones (and thereby avoid getting gifts in return from others that are mostly useless for you!). Travel less; Don't spend on latest fashions that fade away too soon. Spend more quality time with your near and dear ones at home rather than wasting time with friends and colleagues at pubs and bars. Do not move with friends whose lifestyles and spending patterns are a class above you. Don't compare yourself with others and try to imitate their lifestyle.

Get rid of bad habits

Smoking, drinking, eating junk food at odd hours, betting, spending money on lottery, gambling - there are umpteen things that we get hooked on but find too difficult to wriggle ourselves out of. A strong mental determination is needed to come out of them, but if we are successful, this alone can contribute the greatest in saving money fast.

CHAPTER THIRTY-SIX

The Effects of Wasteful Spending

Hot money in hand makes different people behave in different ways. There are misers who would never love to part with the money; there are calculated spenders who plan and account every penny they spend to avoid wasteful spending; and there are spendthrifts who feel restless till the money in hand is exhausted quickly in useful or wasteful ways.

It is not practical to ensure a 100% waste-free spending of money always. We all have our weaknesses, temptations and instantaneous loss of common sense that lead us to spend money once a while in wasteful channels and we regret later for having succumbed to such momentary weaknesses. A patient understanding of the effects of wasteful spending will definitely keep us in good stead when we come across another temptation. Let us now see some such effects of wasteful spending

Unwanted accumulation of junk

Many of us spend wastefully on short living, latest electronic gadgets, latest fashion wear and decorative and eye-catching artifacts. Anything too latest has a tendency to become outdated too soon. What is prestigious to own and boast off today loses its sheen and prestige value tomorrow. Result? We throw them away into the cupboard and go about shamelessly wasting money on newer attractions.

Over a period of time, the house becomes a junkyard. Most of the items have no resale value and they can't be discarded even in garage sales.

Constant stress on earning more money

A penny saved is a penny earned. On the other hand, a penny spent uselessly forces you to work more to earn more – for two reasons: one, you need your pennies for spending on essential things, that you could have obtained if you had not spent them money uselessly; second, your habitual spending on useless things create you a craving for more money for useless spending in future too.

This constant craving for money makes one restless in life. At one end, you want to "enjoy life in full" by spending; at the other end, you slog your life out to earn that extra money. This naturally creates tensions and contradictions in life, leading to loss of mental stability and physical health.

Debt trap

As long as your spendings is within your earning limits and you have a regular saving habit, some amount of wasteful spending can be tolerated. But, if wasteful spending becomes a habit, then over a period of time, spending beyond earning limits becomes an acceptable lifestyle for you. Credit cards come in very handy to lead you to overindulgence. Like an undiagnosed cancer, the debt keeps accumulating in your life and the day will not be far off when you wake up to the dangerous reality of a financial ruin in your life.

Health hazards

Wasteful spending in junk foods, in consuming aerated soft drinks, in dining out with friends, in frequent parties of celebration (say, birth days, valentine days, to celebrate a promotion in office etc) lead you to uncontrolled and undisciplined eating. Poor eating practice is one of the prime causes of health breakdowns.

Getting caught in debt creates lots of mental agony and its consequence shows in physical health. High blood pressure, acidity, peptic ulcer, migraine, physical fatigue etc are some tell-tale signs of loss of physical health on account of mental stress caused by debt.

A very ancient Tamil poem states this: "If a person's expenses exceed income, over a period of time, he loses his respect, loses mental balance, gets tempted to stealing, paves way for a rogue's life in the next seven births, and he tends to look a bad person in the eyes of good people". Hence, beware of wasteful spending.

CHAPTER THIRTY-SEVEN

Organizing your personal finance

Organizing your finance properly is concerned with three things - caring for the present, settling the past burdens and planning for the future; you need discipline, time to be allocated for organizing this work and a reasonable amount of record keeping, paper work (or computer work) and systematic updating for this purpose.

Your existing financial resources and the incoming financial revenues (earnings) have to be properly disbursed in three channels – one, to run your family on a daily basis to cover basic needs of food clothing and shelter; two, to service your past debts and three, to invest and save for the future.

To meet the inevitable spending on food, clothing and shelter and also to a fair extent on additional comforts and luxuries (travel, holidaying, entertainment etc) you must have sufficient income and ideally that income should be more than the expenditure. For organizing your finances on this "present" aspect, you need to keep income and expenditure accounts, draw up budgets for spending and also have the physical and mental discipline to limit your spending within the budget.

Tracking your current financial activities

Keeping an account notebook (either as a physical notebook where you write down or in your PC in the form of a spreadsheet) is a must for this purpose. Your account book should have, other than cash in-hand and cash expense entries, a separate section for recording all your bank transactions. While it is fine that technology has made many things simple (mobile banking, tracking bank accounts through the Internet etc) there is nothing like a written record to make sure that you don't forget any information on checks issued by you or checks received and deposited in a bank. Periodically, your account note book must be tallied with your bank statements.

Tracking your debts

It is important that you have clear written records of your debts, deferred payment advice to credit card firms, monthly installment payments due to you on your hire purchase, home mortgage/ loans etc. It is essential that when you draw up your monthly budget, you make provision for repaying your debts promptly on date so that you are not charged with any penalty nor burdened with excessive debts that can grow unmanageable.

Securing your future

"Let your first expenditure be a saving" so say the wise men. The most important part of organizing your finances is to organize your savings, periodic and one- time investments, purchase and sale of Mutual funds/ shares, investments aimed at tax saving, Insurance plans etc.

Certain websites can be extremely useful in organizing your personal investments and tracking the Return on Investment, current asset values, the extent of capital growth on the investments etc. One such very useful website is "moneycontol.com".

People who are basically lethargic and undisciplined may think that such systematic record keeping and tracking is boring and can potentially rob one of the joy of carefree earning and spending. But if one wants peace of mind and a sense of security on financial standing, properly organizing one's finances and monitoring them through systematic record-keeping is of paramount importance.

-=()=-

CHAPTER THIRTY-EIGHT

Link between Money and Happiness – some musings

Right from childhood we have heard from elders that money cannot buy happiness. During childhood most of us took it with a pinch of salt because we thought when parents have lots of money, they can buy lots of gifts for us and we always felt gifts brought us some joy.

During childhood, our needs were mostly simple; in childhood innocence, the relative costs of goods were mostly non-issues. A marble or a top costing a few pennies owned by a neighborhood poor boy may look too attractive for a rich boy who has a few automatic toy cars worth several dollars. He may even be willing to exchange his toy car for the wooden top!

So, in childhood, possessing something that we loved to have, gave us joy irrespective of the item's worth in money. We also knew another fact of life in childhood at the back of our minds. Whatever that gave us joy had only a transient and relative worth. We were ready to throw away a teddy bear that we carried hugging all day long, the moment we came across a new, more attractive and novel toy!

The source of transient pleasure - money or possessions?

As we grew up and lost our childhood innocence, we also forgot what we learned from the back of our minds about happiness. In childhood, we were willing to throw away things we were formerly attached to; we never calculated their money value. But as grown-ups, we start clinging to our possessions. Even if we have lost the pleasure of our possession, we develop an attachment to them. We think thrice before discarding something because we had spent our hard-earned money acquiring them.

Did the money bring happiness when we originally acquired the possession? It appeared to be so. Did the money ensure the presence of happiness forever in our possession? No, it didn't. Did money act as a hindrance in getting rid of what we no longer consider pleasure-giving? Sometimes it looks like that!

So, it is clear that the pleasure or pain that we associate with something is actually related to our attachment to the possession. But it is our conditioned mindset that tells us that acquiring and possessing gives us pleasure. The more we increase our cravings for such possessions, the more we run around to earn money to afford them.

Does lack of money cause unhappiness?

It seems to be definitely so. A poor man who is always short of money to fill his stomach with 3 square meals a day is definitely unhappy. One who does not have money to buy cloth to protect him from heat or cold is definitely unhappy. Thus a certain amount of money that can ensure the supply of basic human needs of food, clothing, and shelter can definitely ward off unhappiness.

Does excess supply of money ensure happiness?

Obviously not. The needs, wants and greed of a person always seem to grow in proportion to the money he/ she already possesses; with excess money comes the worry to protect it and maintain it; with excess money, one gets used to excessive luxuries and any worry about the likelihood of losing them makes one spend sleepless nights.

Is there happiness in hunting behind money?

For many people, it seems to be so! Businessmen work days and nights losing timely food and sleep to earn more and more money. They build palatial houses, fill them with the best and latest gadgets but they do not find time to relax and enjoy what they painstakingly built. They possess the latest music system but are not gifted with a good music sense or time to sit and relax to enjoy the music!

Is there happiness in hoarding money?

It seems to be so for the category of misers! All their joy lies in accumulating money and seeing a hefty balance in their bank account but any idea of spending the money to enjoy what others generally consider as enjoyment gives them only sorrow!

They are prepared to go any length to sacrifice their comforts, economize their essential needs, deny near and dear ones access to any goodies, just to have the pleasure of accumulating their money in the bank; all their concern is in the future when something may go wrong, at which point of time they think the money they accumulated will be handy. Sri Ramakrishna Pramahamsa says that the accumulated wealth of misers would only get squandered away by unworthy sons, in medical treatment, in court litigation, or by burglary. So, it looks like the accumulated money of a miser seems to have the potential to bring transient happiness to those who squander it!

The secret behind money and happiness

A happy-go-lucky man, middle-aged, who always seemed to be joyful, shared the secret of his happiness with those who were curious to learn from him, as follows:

"I have somehow grasped the fact right from childhood that it is simple living that brings happiness; I have made it a point in my life to make consistent efforts to simplify life; be it food, clothing or shelter. Be it work, materialistic comforts or travel.

"Make your needs less. Shun luxuries. Never compare yourself with anyone else in your peer group. Consequently, your need for money becomes less. When you don't need money to possess goodies that you don't really need, you lose any idea of linking money with pleasure. So, you don't have to run around and exert yourself to earn more and more money than you really need! When the pain of acquiring money is removed, you have the pleasure of leading a peaceful life."

Any takers?

-=()=-

CHAPTER THIRTY-NINE

Contentment, Money and Happiness

Happiness is a state of mind and it does not depend on money, though many of us chase money with the hope that its abundance can bring us happiness. But will happiness bring you money? It requires a deeper analysis to get the right answer to this question.

Can you consider remaining contended equivalent to being happy? Can you consider remaining peaceful equivalent to being happy? To a large extent, yes. If the word "happiness" gives you a mental picture of a wide mouthed laugh, shaking your limbs in a jig, or lifting up your arms to cry "hooray!", then "contentment" or "peace" does not fit the picture.

But, when we say "contented" or "peaceful", we get a mental picture of a serene smile, a relaxed atmosphere of absence of hype and hoopla, and a sense of well being, soothing to the body and mind. When you meet a saintly person or when you are inside an ancient church or a temple where the crowd is absent and everything around is serene, you feel a sense of peace and contentment; that feel, at that moment, looks far more valuable and worthy to you than the noisy party that you attended the previous night, which, nevertheless was enjoyable to you at that point of time.

Now you know the nuances behind being happy and being content. If being happy is like the sea at the shores where the waves lash out, being contented is like the sea farther away from the shore, far more calm and free from turbulence.

For a contented person, the needs and wants are very limited. He is more comfortable eating simple home food than eating out at exotic restaurants. A simple dress, decent in looks and comfortable to wear, that can protect his modesty and also from the vagaries of heat and cold, is good enough for him and he has no charm for the latest fashion or premium garments. A contented person is happier to live in a rented house than to live in his own house that he could buy only with a heavy mortgage, which can push him deeply into a debt trap.

A contented person has no joy in spending money to give costly gifts to others, nor does he enjoy receiving gifts from others that he may not have any utility or value.

So, when a person develops contentment, he is quite happy with what he has, what he does and what he earns. His need and dependence on money gets drastically reduced. We all know that money saved is money earned. So, such a happy person truly "makes money".

CHAPTER FORTY

Painless Ways to Save Money

Money saved is money earned. The moment we have some excess money in our hands, the first instinct in most of us is to spend it. While spending on basic needs is obviously a necessity, spending on extravaganza is not. But it's always the extravaganza that tempts us to spend our money on, as they seem to have better potential to give us instant gratification and short term pleasures.

In the present day of seeking instant gratification in every aspect of life and the culture of Credit Card that leads the way towards it, many of us meekly get into a debt trap. Once you are caught in unbridled spending habits, the tendency to save takes a back seat. Hence, saving money must be inculcated as an enforced habit in us. Here are some ways to save money:

Let your first expenditure be a saving

This is a famous and pregnant statement. The first habit you should develop when you start earning on your own is a strict discipline to put a small percentage of your income into savings on the very day of your receiving the paycheck. For that, you should open a Recurring Deposit account in your Bank and give standing instructions to the Bankers to debit a specified amount automatically from your Checking Account to your Recurring Deposit account on your pay-day.

Thus you will have only a truncated amount for withdrawal and you will automatically develop a discipline to curtail your expenditure to the available amount.

Never utilize the "minimum amount payable" facility in your credit card

Living within your means is a time-tested and age-old wisdom which is unfortunately forgotten in today's Credit Card culture. What you buy using a Credit Card should be payable IN FULL by you when the bill arrives from the Credit Card firm. If you get lured by the "Minimum Amount due Now", it paves the way for accumulation of debt.

If the object of desire can be purchased by you only through installment by utilizing the "Minimum Pay-out Money", DO NOT SUCCUMB to the temptation of purchase. By bringing in this self-control, you may lose short-term pleasures, but you will enjoy long term peace.

If you find it too difficult to curtail your temptation to go on a spending spree just because the credit card is there, you can think of an enforced discipline on you - use a debit card and discard your credit card!

If you have the habit of wielding multiple credit cards, keep just one and get rid of all the others.

Never indulge in unplanned purchases

Let everyone in the family know that there is an upper limit for spending on gifts. Do not encourage your partner or your children to pester you or cajole you to get a costlier item than what you have budgeted, particularly when festival and gifting seasons like Christmas arrives.

Avoid last minute purchases

If you are purchasing goods and gifts during a festival season, why should you get tensed up amidst surging crowds, irritable salesmen, hiked up prices and long and winding queues? Why don't you shop much earlier before prices get hiked up to rob the last minute shoppers? Better still, why not shop comfortably sitting relaxed just in front of your computer by purchasing straight away on-line?

Remember: A trip to the prestigious shopping mall with the entire family in your car will add lots of peripheral expenditure like cost of gas, impulsive but unwanted purchases, in snacks, drinks and other refreshments, which you can totally avoid by your purchases through the internet. You can always look for cheaper auctions too on these sites.

Try second hand items at Garage sales

What one person wants to throw away could be a treasure for another. Why don't you try to visit garage sales in the neighborhood if you have a particular requirement in your mind? Perhaps you can save considerable money, if only your hunt becomes successful.

Buy in bulk, if consumption and storage are not issues

In India, our grandmothers practiced a habit of buying pulses, tamarind (which is an essential ingredient of cooking in south India), Chili and other spices at seasons when they will be available at the cheapest prices and in plenty. They will procure their stock practically for an entire year and store them in bulky containers, suitably protecting them from moths and rodents. This way, our grandmothers saved lots of money.

Though the present generation in urban locales has practically forgotten this wisdom, it is still practiced in rural India. But we can always practice a toned-down version of this habit. You can always buy much larger packs (like detergents, shampoo, toothpastes, energy drinks etc) where buying in bulkier quantities saves you money. Instead of planning your budgets every month, you can always plan for budgets on these items for a stretch of 2 to 3 months.

Reduce eating out

No explanation is needed on this advice. Eating at home is far more economical, healthy and nutritious.

Travel less

If your place of residence is much closer to your place of work, you not only save quite considerably on conveyance, but you can save time and strain of traveling too.

Reduce frequency of holiday trips

Holiday trips are obviously the greatest money drainers. If you have the habit of going on a holiday trip every year, start making them every alternate year.

Downgrade your mode of transport

If the distance you have to travel can be walked, avoid your bicycle. If the distance to be covered can be done by cycling, avoid using a scooter/ motor bike. If you can do a trip with a scooter/motorbike, avoid taking a car. If you can go by public transport (bus/ suburban train/ tube rail) don't take your car.

Talk less over mobile phone

It's a very obvious but an extremely difficult proposition for most. Right?

Change to a cheaper locality

If you live in a rented house, house rent takes up a major chunk of your income. Instead of residing in a costly and prestigious locality, if you can shift your residence to a suburb where house rents are much cheaper (provided you have a cheap mass-transport facility like suburban train service to commute to your office), you can save a considerable amount.

You may think that not all the modes of saving money discussed above are painless. The more you get used to certain avoidable and unwanted luxuries, you may initially find it somewhat painful if you have to come out of them. But the question of saving money would not have come unless excessive spending or lack of bank balance has already started hurting you. Before the problem snowballs into a major pain in life, you can always wake up and save money, tolerating some minor pains in the bargain!

CHAPTER FORTY-ONE

Why a Sound Household Budget is Key to Debt Reduction

Debt comes to you through three channels.

One, you have borrowed money from a financing source for a specific and well intended purpose which you have to pay back in installments as per clearly agreed terms and conditions. Your monthly pay back commitment is crystal clear; it is mostly by virtue of your earning potential that you have obtained your loans. Example: A home loan or a car loan.

Two, you have borrowed some amount from an acquaintance to tide over an unexpected emergency situation. You have to pay it back, with or without interest, within a time frame mutually agreed by you and your financier.

Three, you keep spending joyfully through your credit cards and when the monthly bills arrive, you opt to pay "the minimum amount payable" and take the rest of the amount into credit, to be paid back later as per the terms of credit card.

When it comes to making a sound household budget and understanding its influence on debt reduction, all the three types of debts we discussed above have a strong bearing.

In your household budget, your committed monthly loan repayment amount from the first type of loans will be one of the clear and prominent items in the list. You cannot wish away this expenditure. This expenditure is like other fixed and non-negotiable items in your budget like your house rent.

When it comes to repaying your casual/ unexpected borrowings falling into the type two category, perhaps you would get tempted to postpone the repayment, because, after all, you got it from a friend who might not sit on your head to get it repaid. Though such an attitude may help you in reducing a yawning gap between income that is less and expenditure that is more, it has every potential to keep you under debt trap for long.

When you fail to repay something that somebody loaned to you in good faith expecting you to repay honestly sooner, you start compromising on your principles and values. Never make that mistake. Any such casual borrowings must be repaid promptly. You must include it in your expenditure item in your budget. If you can't repay it in one go, you must break it into a couple of installments and be sincere to pay it off every month without being asked.

Now when it comes to the third category of loans, namely uncontrolled spending through credit cards by relying on the deferred payment option given to you by the credit card firm, it is the most potent weapon that can ground you into a debt trap with a very huge interest burden in the long run.

It is in the above category that your budgeting and discipline to sticking to budgeted spending plays a major role in debt reduction.

Every element in your budget, be it food, drinks, clothing, gas, car maintenance expenses, entertainment, gifts to others, medicines - every single element must be scrutinized and monitored to avoid overspending. Every attempt must be made to economize the expenditure on them.

If you visit a shopping mall, carry your budgeted purchase list and never get tempted to buy anything unbudgeted.

Your aim in using credit cards must be to pay off the entire amount that comes in the credit card bill on the due date promptly.

To develop this singular discipline, preparing a sound household budget helps a lot. It is not just by preparing the budget but by sticking to its limits that you pave the way for debt reduction.

-=()=-

CHAPTER FORTY-TWO

Debt-free life – Can you make it possible?

In today's credit card culture, this question "how to live without borrowed money" may seem absurd and impractical. Individuals, business houses, industries and Government - practically the life of every activity in this world seems to run on credits, with a generous dose of borrowed money.

When the balance between borrowing and repayment gets skewed beyond a degree, the system of credits and debits crumble and the damage it does to the money flow is too heavy. This is what the recent subprime crisis in the US taught us.

Why does the life of most of us turn to be dependent on borrowed money? Let us ignore the cases where poverty is the prime cause. Where poverty is not there, where the basic human needs of food, clothing and shelter are adequately met, why do people still lead lives with borrowed money?

What makes people go on a borrowing spree?

The reasons are many, but the predominant cause can be traced to comparing ourselves with peers and with those who are at higher social status than us.

The next cause is the tendency to show off. Third reason is unbridled greed to "enjoy" life to "the fullest" with a mad belief that living a life of satiating sensual desires by hook or crook is the goal of life.

The next reason is to lead a life without any inner development, to lead a life in tune with the rest of the mass in the world, with no conscious self-analysis about what one really and essentially needs or does not need for a happy and peaceful existence in this world.

Result? People spend money more and more on things that they may have no need for, on things that are simply far beyond their true financial status, on things that are going to give them short term thrills but end them up with long term pain.

Mindset after borrowing money

Living on borrowed money initially may not be too burdensome. As one proceeds life in the same way, the burden mounts more and more. Sensitive and self-respecting people feel miserable at some point of their life for leading such a life and they may wake up to the ugly reality of their horrid financial status. They may try to fight out their position by sacrificing their comforts and do everything they could possibly do to wipe out their loans and regain their lost prestige.

Strangely, there are also people who get used to living far above their means on borrowed money and they gradually lose the sense of guilt in leading such a life; beyond a stage, they get immune to pressures, litigations, loss of respect in society and even end up in insolvency but still not feel anything bad about it. According to CBS News (see Video), about 2600 Americans are currently filing bankruptcy every day. It is a revelation on the sorry state of affairs prevailing in the present day.

The above, second category of people can not be easily educated on the silent happiness of living a debt-free life.

Living without borrowing - is it possible?

For those, who know the perils of living off borrowed money, is it really possible in today's lifestyle to lead a life without borrowing money, without engaging in deferred payments or without getting into installment payments in personal lives?

Yes. It is possible; but it requires a lateral shift in our lifestyle, personal ethos, beliefs, principles and values.

Why should one think of a debt-free life?

Why should anyone ever think of leading a life without loans? It's because the innate spirituality in us tells us that a peaceful life is more satisfying in the long run than a life filled with thrills and instant gratification attained beyond our means.

It tells us that a life where you are not answerable to anybody on your financial matters is a life truly blessed; it is a life where a good night's sleep night after night is assured. Spirituality tells us that a simple life with simple needs is far more wholesome and satisfying in the long run than life filled with grandiose and extravaganza.

Tips for living a debt-free life

Don't compare

Avoid comparing yourself with your peers, colleagues, friends and relatives. Your life is yours. Your lifestyle really need not reflect on someone else's tastes, preferences and needs. Tell yourself firmly that if at all some people are going to "accept" you in their circle based on their perceived status, you need not really value or respect their company.

Know your "don't wants"

Be very clear on things you do not want in life; on things that are attractive to so many others, but not really attractive or of value to you. Example: If golden or diamond jewelry is least attractive to you and if you consider investing money on them is a waste, why should you ever spend money on them or borrow money to accumulate and hoard them in the bank lockers?

There can be umpteen examples on things that need not be attractive to you, but the society by and large spends lots of money: Holidaying by traveling to exotic destinations, buying the latest model premium car, eating in prestigious restaurants, buying the costliest branded footwear or fashion garments, engaging in hobbies that are very costly to your wallet.

Watch your bad habits

Smoking, drinking exotic champagnes, frequent partying with friends and colleagues, restless wandering and traveling, unnecessary eating out when you can eat more healthily at home, excessive drinking of coffee, tea and aerated soft drinks, love for gobbling up junk food and snacks in between meal times, spending on latest electronic gadgets unmindful of their true utility value, giving unwanted gifts to others just to impress them, addiction to shopping spree - there are umpteen such bad habits in us that tempt us to swipe our credit cards at the drop of a hat, without thinking on the evil consequences.

Spend in cash - use the credit card to the least

When we physically touch our hard-earned money and hand it over to somebody else or part with it once for all, we feel a small pinch in our hearts! When you see our money flowing out easily from your wallet, you get worried. You stop to think "Am I overspending? Could I avoid this expenditure?" It is not the case with spending through credit cards.

If you must use your credit card, you must ensure that when the due date of payment arrives, you have adequate money in your bank to pay it in full straight away. Never get tempted to pay "the minimum amount payable now" that the Credit card firm tempts you with.

Save money before you buy

Be it a purchase for Christmas, a capital purchase like furniture for your house or a piece of gold jewelry that your wife loves to have, you must first earn that amount and save it. Then spend it and be free from any worry.

It would be highly ideal if you can extend this principle to buy more costly purchases like a car. If a car is a must, can you settle for a second hand car which you can purchase straight away from your accumulated savings?

Simplify life

Walk if you can bicycle. Go by bicycle if you can avoid a motorbike. Go by motorbike if you can avoid a car. Go by railroad instead of taking a flight if the distance permits. Have just one TV for the family instead of one per living room. Have just one car for the family. Have just one credit card for the family. Live in a rented house instead of buying your own house and then getting burdened by a huge home loan which cannot be serviced easily with your present income.

All said and done, we are all social creatures and we get easily disturbed by what the society thinks about us or what we imagine the society thinking about us! Living a highly simplified life may appear too difficult and infra-dig for many of us. But if we are gritty and determined, we can not only live a life free of worries about debts, we can also truly enjoy by personal experience the hidden joy behind simple living.

-=()=-

Why Invest in Land

Investing in land is one of the best forms of investment when looked from several angles. If you invest in shares, it is highly volatile, subject to the sentiments and vagaries of the market and most of the times it is as good as gambling. If you invest in any other safer forms like fixed deposits, mutual funds, debentures etc, the return on investment is at the best nominal.

Investment in gold is traditionally considered quite secure and the appreciation of gold has always been nominal, but reasonable. But investment in gold cannot bring spectacular returns.

However, investing in land, if done judiciously at the right place and right time, the return on investment is bound to be fantastic in the long run.

Investing in agricultural land

Investment in land can be done with several motives. An agriculturist investing in arable land has scope for regular returns off the agricultural produce from the land and also as a long term investment on an appreciable asset. For rural people traditionally involved in agriculture, possession of owned land is a matter of social status and prestige. Even if the villagers are not getting adequate agricultural returns from their lands over a period of time owing to reasons like, floods, large scale pest attack, draught, low produce, excess produce (that outstrips demand) etc., still buying and owning land continues to be a matter of pride and prestige amidst rural peer group.

Owning a house in your own land

Amidst urbanites, owning a home of one's own is always a dream to be fulfilled in life. However, owning a piece of land that's your own and building an exclusive house on your own on that land may not be a dream that can be fulfilled for many people. For people with limited investible funds and repayment capacity, owning a flat in a multistoried residential building is an affordable compromise.

But ownership of a flat is nowhere comparable with the ownership of land. The flat owner has little piece of land that he can claim his own. A person investing in a piece of sub-urban land, that is perhaps half of the area of a big, owned flat in the urban locality is still a better investor in the long run. Even if the person cannot realize the dream of building his own home in that piece of land, the land is very much available, perhaps to his grandson, to build a house of his own after two generations from now. At that point of time, the piece of land would be prohibitively costly for the grandson, if he were to buy something similar on his own!

Thus a grandpa of hand-to-mouth existence today could gift an unimaginably luxurious piece of land to his grandson! This scenario is possible only if one invests in land and not in a flat.

CHAPTER FORTY-FOUR

Reflections – Finding True Happiness – Moderation is the key

Every one of us seeks pleasure, joy, and merriment. But in reality, we almost always encounter pairs of opposites: pleasure-pain, joy-sorrow, merry-worry. Hindu philosophy emphasizes that they are in reality, package deals - if you buy one, the other is given free - immediately, sooner or later! The oft-quoted statement is "they are like both sides of the same coin".

Is 'happiness' different from 'pleasure', 'joy' or 'merry'? Yes! What is the opposite of happiness? It is unhappiness - meaning absence of happiness. Unhappiness need not necessarily mean sorrow, pain or worry; It simply means absence of happiness - that's all.

Does it mean that there are some ways and means of enjoyment available that need not be attached with a bitter, opposing counterpart? Yes, says Hindu philosophy. But there are 2 conditions for getting such happiness. One is moderation and the other is detachment or dispassion.

How do we get enjoyment, pleasure etc.? One channel is through our five senses. The other channel is through our ego.

Hinduism strongly says that seeking pleasures through senses without moderation will lead to getting pains through the same channels. Let us just analyze only two of the five sense pleasures here:

Food is essential for a healthy living; you have taste buds to enjoy your food. But if you allow your love for taste over-power you, you start getting trouble though your food.

Sex is necessary for procreation; need for sex is a biological and emotional need. But if you allow your craze for sex to overpower you, you start getting trouble though your sex organ as well as through your mind.

This is how God has given us sources of enjoyment with strings attached to them. That is his divine play. God enjoys, as it were, seeing his creation getting more and more entrapped in pain, directly in proportion to their craving for pleasure. This aspect is called Maya in Hinduism.

Then, how do you get happiness? By enjoying, with moderation.

Moderation in food

Eat moderately. Eat in time. Do not get tempted to eat when offered un-time.

Restrict the items that tempt you the most - deep fried items, sweets, spicy food, and junk food. If 3 helpings of desserts will satisfy your palate, restrict to one.

Instead of gulping like a dog, chew more, relish and then swallow. By practicing this, you will find that you are able to derive the true joy of eating, develop a better sense of taste and be able to restrict excess consumption. That is happiness for you!

Once a while, leave your stomach empty. Skip supper once or twice a week. Instead, just take a couple of fruits and a glass of milk. Over a period of time you will get happiness through this skipping, by the enhanced feeling of wellbeing.

Moderation in the case of sex

Restrict your sex strictly to your married partner. To start enjoying sex, wait untill you get married.

Moderate your frequency of having sex. Do not concentrate on the sex-act alone. Enjoy the paraphernalia - The togetherness, the sweet-nothings, the touch, the embrace, the cuddling, and the foreplay. Relax, prolong and derive happiness.

As you consciously reduce your frequency and enjoy the relaxed way of having sex, you will find that your sense of appreciation of the sexual pleasure sharpens - the happiness is more than the momentary thrill. The path becomes as enjoyable as the destination. The carnal desire gets replaced by love.

Abstain from sex for a week or so, even when your partner is very much together with you, once in a while. When the decision is a conscious one, with both the partners discussing and agreeing to, you will find that the happiness increases multi-fold when you are together again after the self-imposed abstinence.

Likewise, you can extend the concept to other sense pleasures too.

Now, coming to deriving pleasure through our ego. We get ego satisfaction in so many ways

- by acquiring more and more wealth
- by acquiring more knowledge
- by acquiring power to dominate, to subjugate others
- by indulging in creative activity (music, dance, painting, sports etc.)
- by searching behind appreciation, name and fame and in case of lesser mortals, just notoriety

As predictable, you will have opposites coming together to torment you.

- Behind wealth, there is worry to protect it and the lurking fear of losing it.
- Behind knowledge there is an ever expanding space of ignorance

- Behind a creative activity like say, sports, there is injury; there is the pain of defeat.
- Behind your fame, there are always bitter critics; People's tastes change and there is always someone else to edge you out of the limelight.

Only by practicing moderation, only by taming your egoistic needs, will you be able to get happiness. Just watch the people around you. Who is happier - a very egoistic person or one is far less egoistic? Whom do you love to move with? A boastful, proud, authoritative and pushy person or the one who is humble, unassuming, someone who has the capacity to laugh at himself?

From moderation to detachment / dispassion

Does moderation alone give a sustainable happiness? Not entirely. You can moderate consumption, but perhaps cannot conquer the mental craving. This craving remains in you as a seed and it grows to a strong tree in moments of weakness. And it creates attachment towards objects of enjoyment.

Attachment is the cause of misery. Your attachment to smoking, drinking etc gradually turns into addiction. Your attachment to the objects of desire turns into greed, possessiveness and selfishness. The Bhagawad Gita says "from attachment comes longing; from longing, anger grows; from anger delusion comes; from delusion comes loss of good thoughts; from the loss of good thoughts comes loss of discrimination; finally comes ruin" (2-62,63).

If you can develop detachment and renounce pleasure-seeking, you will be saved from the associated pain. The happiness of drinking a good cup of coffee is sustainable, if you are totally free from the craving for coffee.

If a woman frees herself from an acute sense of possessiveness towards her husband or children, to that extent she is freed from the pains of rupture in relationship and can enjoy mental peace.

The happiness derived from any pursuit lingers longer if only we know when to retire gracefully. If only we can develop utter detachment towards our body, even death becomes enjoyable. The purpose of any religion is to elevate a man's mindset to such an exalted level.

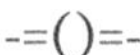

CHAPTER FORTY-FIVE

How to Maintain Good Health as you get Older

Getting older is the law of nature; a machinery long used tends to wear more and also breakdown more frequently. That is also the law of nature. For an old machinery to keep running, plant Engineers know very well that a good preventive maintenance, regular lubrication and running of the machine at a less than optimum work load are essential.

The same principles are applicable to older people to maintain good health in the long run! Let us see what these "maintenance engineer's practices" are, as applicable to old age health.

Preventive maintenance

Old age invariably brings in ailments like high blood pressure, body aches, diabetes, rheumatism etc to lots of people. Most of these health problems can be successfully managed and the body well "maintained", though such complaints cannot be totally wished away. To keep them under control, taking proper and regular medicines as prescribed by the doctors, sticking to prescribed diet and exercises and also visiting doctors periodically to check the status of affairs and readjust medication will be necessary.

Following a disciplined regimen in all these practices will prevent the ailments becoming serious and out of control. In other words, good preventive maintenance will avoid a serious breakdown.

Lubricate regularly in right quantity

Though lubrication by itself may become a part of preventive maintenance of machinery, its importance requires special emphasis. Eating healthy, wholesome food, with adequate balance in all nutrients and vitamins in old age is akin to lubrication of machinery. While excess lubrication may not cause serious problems in machinery, it is not the case with eating at old age!

As one grows older, food intake must be gradually reduced, without compromising, however, on the nutrition content. Caloric requirements become less as one ages. Any excessive intake of calories results in accumulation of fat. A fat body at old age is a real cause for health troubles.

At old age, it is not possible to burn excess fat through exercise. Hence the only means available to avoid putting on fat is to reduce the caloric intake. This is one habit that has to be cultivated very consciously as one grows old.

Reduce working

People who love work and who have always been proud of working without eying the clock would find this advice hard to digest. Be active. No second question on that. But be more relaxed too. Some people refuse to accept getting older, but their bodies do not share their view!

Brain activity, working of motor nerves, reflex action etc do deteriorate as one ages. Naturally, whether people do predominantly mental working (like designing, computer programming etc) or predominantly physical working, their efficiency and capabilities slow down as they age. Keeping your working standards of yester-years and trying to live up to those, out of sheer enthusiasm, can potentially cause trouble to the physical and mental health.

Hence one must learn to retire gracefully. Start delegating more; give responsibility to youngsters and learn to relax; reduce your high standards of performance.

It goes without saying that bad habits started at young age (smoking, alcoholism, drug addiction etc) cannot be continued at old age; in youth, the body has the capacity to withstand abuse. But as one grows older, a previously abused body tends to degenerate more quickly. Old habits must be weaned away gradually but definitely, if one wants good health at an older age.

Do not allow rusting

This is the extreme end of dragging things too far on what we discussed previously. Machinery, however old, has to be ensured to be fit and in running condition; if they are disused, they rust quickly and become fit only for the junkyard sooner.

Old age should not be used as an excuse to avoid doing mental or physical activity altogether. Sloth will lead to generation of more ailments at old age. For good physical fitness at old age, regular walking should be done; walking is by far the best form of exercise most natural for the human body for all ages. Reading books, solving crossword puzzles or Sudoku puzzles can be continued easily right up to ripe old age.

To summarize, to maintain good health as you get older, one has to eat healthy, eat less quantity, exercise (walk) regularly, keep unavoidable ailments under firm control and keep oneself engaged in physical and mental activities at moderate level.

CHAPTER FORTY-SIX

What's more Important -- your Career or your Family?

Extremely few people ever want to live unmarried. Most people get married/ want to get married in order to have a loving relationship with the spouse, have a nice family, rear children, have basic comforts in life, enjoy some luxuries, have a peaceful retired life and have your life and comforts taken care of by children at old age.

Yes; there are hiccups that happen in married life; husband-wife relationship gets strained; lots of fights happen; Children become disobedient; children go astray; loans eat up your life; children leave abroad to chart their own life and discard parents at old age. But, people still really want to cling to family life and derive some joy out of it. They get divorced because the relationship between the spouses gets beyond repair; they want to get remarried because they want the love and intimacy with the spouse as a basic need in a family set up. The children are to be taken care of, either born at previous wedlock or at new wedlock.

Thus everything revolves around family. The very purpose of working and earning money is predominantly to run the family. When the family life is smooth and cordial, when there is love and care existing, then every strain of working in a job and earning money becomes more meaningful.

On the other hand, think of the situation where career becomes more important. When one becomes career oriented, one's prime attention goes in satisfying the boss, working for long hours in the office or even on holidays to prove one's ambition, worth and commitment by giving one's best to the office but only of secondary importance to family life. In such a life, there is every chance that the family relationships get strained, communication between spouses gets bad, parent-children relationship deteriorates and so on.

Ultimately, whatever the purpose of having a job and earning money gets distorted and skewed because the original purpose (family life) goes on deteriorating on account of chasing a career!

It is like a snake swallowing its own tail in order to satiate its hunger!

So, family is more important than career.

This is my firm conviction. This is true for both men and women.

Women and Career - Listen to your heart please

All said and done, God has made women primarily to be mothers first and foremost, than anything other role she can play. Right from puberty, a woman's body is devised and developed by nature to culminate her growth into motherhood. Even the most nymphomaniac of a woman, once becomes a mother, feels a sense of fulfillment in her life through motherhood rather than sexuality. There may be exceptions to this idea, but for the vast majority of women, this statement is true. It is not just the body of a woman that is predisposed for motherhood. Her very psyche, emotions and sentiments are built around motherhood.

If you are a career woman who has to leave children behind to rush to work, what does your heart say? Do you feel pain to leave your little children behind to fend for themselves while you slog it out at the office for the sake of intellectual gratification, self esteem, peer group pressure or for the lure of money that gets you luxuries? Does your conscience prick? If so, it is time to listen to your heart and to your conscience, rather than to your head.

Psychiatrists say that whatever love, affection, company, and cuddling you give to your children, give them below their 10th age. Beyond that age, these things do not matter too much for the children. Your love and affection get deeply imprinted in their psyche for the rest of their lives.

Personally, I feel, every child radiates godly qualities till the age of 4. Every moment you, as a mother, spend with the child till this age enhances and embellishes the very quality and worth of your life; the bliss of this togetherness with 'God' cannot be explained by mere words. As the children grow up above 4, they lose their innocence, start acquiring worldly knowledge and start developing their individual personalities gradually. The divinity in them fades away, only to be replaced by human qualities.

If you have an option to be with your children full-time during this period, it is the best you can get in your life and the best you can give to your children in their life. If your mind and conscience goads you to accept this choice, go ahead - forget extra money, forget the ego satisfaction that a career gives, forget peer group pressure, forget status comparison with others - live a life on your own terms to acquire what you feel is the best for your soul.

-=()=-

CHAPTER FORTY-SEVEN

How to age with dignity

When you meet an elderly citizen who is quite known to you, what sort of feeling do you develop at the back of your mind? Is it a sense of respect or one of disgust? Do you feel humble while talking to him not because "he /she is aged and hence needs to be shown respect" but because you really feel that way in front of him/her?

Our reaction ultimately boils down to one simple fact – how dignified the old person is in his/her demeanor.

In Indian traditional wisdom, it is said that as a person becomes older and older, the one characteristic he/she should develop more and more is detachment. This detachment covers physical, emotional, intellectual and social bondages. Further, attachment to the world should get converted to attachment towards God. The more one ages developing these qualities, the more dignified he/she becomes.

In the above light, we shall now see how to develop the qualities for aging with dignity:

Do not attempt to look younger than your age

Such advice may shock many women in the west, because the desire to look young and sexy far beyond youth seems to preoccupy the minds of many women (and some men, too). Remaining healthy, physically fit and fighting against obesity are fine and necessary, but fighting against normal graying of hair, wrinkles on the face, propping up the breasts by women through plastic surgery, etc. are quite unnecessary.

Behave decently with the opposite sex

Whatever a woman does to look far younger than her true age mostly never cuts ice in the eyes of men. When such women try to look sexier too, they totally lose their dignity and even become laughing stocks.

The same applies to some older men who shamelessly ogle young girls and try valiantly to come down to their levels and behave like a dog-in-heat to impress them!

A father of a girl of twenty should a display fatherly demeanor with his daughter's friends, even though his innate and not-yet-subdued sexual urges may tempt him to behave more like a man getting attracted towards the opposite sex.

Get rid of possessiveness over children

Western society seems to be better developed with this quality than eastern society as seen in India. While parents should watch their children till they are in their teen age and be highly responsible for their conduct and character, parents should gracefully loosen their grip on their children once they become adults. Beyond that stage, their relationship with the children should become more like a trustworthy friend.

A mother's attachment towards her children generally continues to remain strong in the emotional plane even far beyond the children's teen age. Possessiveness is a negative force that stealthily remains attached behind a mother's love and many times this possessiveness has a tendency to affect the good conjugal relationship of her children with their spouses.

To age with dignity, parents should carefully watch their possessive mindset and allow their children to chart their course in life fairly independently once they start earning. At the same time, they need not resign from acting as a confidant and guide when the offspring seek help and support.

Parents who rejoice seeing their sons and daughters leading happy married lives and ensure excellent relationships with their son-in-laws, daughter-in-laws and their parents, too, look highly dignified in the eyes of society.

Retire gracefully

A person normally achieves most things in life – good status in society, power and position in his/her profession, enjoying goodies, comforts and authority by the time he/she reaches the age of retirement. But, many people dread retirement because they are too attached to all these and afraid of losing their self-importance after retirement.

But the very concept of retirement has been necessary in society because the younger generation should have the opportunity to achieve higher positions and the aged ones do tend to get slack, inefficient and out of sync with modern trends in technology and lifestyle. Those who refuse to retire gracefully lose respect from the younger generation.

Retiring gracefully and charting a new, purposeful and satisfying lifestyle after retirement goes a long way in aging with dignity.

Be financially self-supporting and independent

By the time one retires, a person should be totally free from debt, should have built up enough savings and resources for supporting oneself and spouse for the rest of old age. Simplifying lifestyle, changing and economizing spending habits, etc. are to be cultivated consciously. Elders who leave debts to their children and who have to totally depend on their children's money for their sustenance will not be able to lead a dignified life at old age.

Be health conscious but do not make a fetish about health

By proper food control, exercise and self discipline, elders should take care of their health very well. Children naturally frown at elders who keep complaining about their health. Some elders tend to read too much literature about diseases and their symptoms and they tend to imagine the existence of such ailments in their bodies.

Some elders tend to exaggerate their ill health and love visiting doctors and gobbling up medicines; they use real or imagined ailments to gain sympathy from their offspring. Such tendencies are obviously detrimental to aging with dignity.

Don't be a bore

One of the despicable qualities in most of the elders is their pride in past laurels – real or imagined. The moment a hapless visitor greets them, they would like to catch him as a prey to talk endlessly about their past, the achievements they made, the adoration they received and the respect they commanded.

Virtually every old person believes that the world was so good and great in yester years and everything has changed topsy-turvy in the present generation. Many old people never get tired of finding fault with others. Old persons feel they are qualified for giving unsolicited advice and the younger generation takes to their heels upon encountering such persons.

Obviously, any old person who talks less about himself/herself but is an avid listener to the younger generation gets respect and love from them.

Contribute to social welfare

The post-retirement period is best for reformatting your lifestyle and making it tuned more toward the welfare of society. By taking part in church/ temple oriented spiritual activities or by associating oneself with non-governmental philanthropic activities, a retired person can spend his time and energy fruitfully for the welfare of society.

Develop detachment

This is one sterling and singular quality that makes an old person respectable to everyone. As you grow older, detach yourself from the attractions of money, wealth, possessions and antiques. Detach yourself from expecting respect and reverence from others.

Detach yourself from expecting others to keep you informed of all the family matters and issues. Do not expect others to consult you and seek "your valuable counsel" for everything. Shower love on your grandchildren without expecting anything in return from them.

Engage yourself in developing spiritual qualities through religious austerities, by practicing yoga, japa (chanting God's name), meditation, etc. Make sure to understand that engaging in such activities are meant to elevate your spiritual stature to a higher level and they are never meant to build your egotism to project yourself as a "highly pious and spiritual old person who has to be revered by all."

Aging is the reality of life and it culminates in death one day. How to age gracefully and with dignity is one of the challenges of life that everyone should face and succeed at.

-=(End)=-

About The Author

C.V. Rajan (Sandeepika)

C.V. Rajan is a retired Engineer and an ex-design consultant, now living with his wife in the Ashram at Amritapuri, Kerala, spending his retired life in quest of spirituality under the holy feet of Amma, Sadguru Mata Amritanandamayi.

Writing as a hobby started in him at the age of 20 and he became a regular short story writer in popular Tamil magazines during the seventies and eighties. He wrote with a pen-name Sandeepika.

As his interest turned to spirituality in his late thirties, he became an avid reader of the lives and teachings of Kanchi Maha Swamigal, Swami Chinmayananda, Sri Ramakrishna Paramahamsa, Bhagwan Ramana Maharshi, Swami Sivananda Saraswathi, Papa Ramadas and his sadguru Mata Amritanandamayi (Amma).

In his early fifties, his Tamil articles started appearing in Sri Ramakrishna Vijayam magazine. He also started writing in English on the Web at various blog sites on a variety of subjects like Hinduism, spirituality, life & living, Indian culture, Small business management and so on. He contributed in the translation works at Ramakrishna Math (English-Tamil) and currently does it at Mata Amritanandamayi Math (Tamil-Malayalam-English).

In his website hinduismwayoflife.com, C.V. Rajan has been consolidating and sharing all his writings on Hinduism under a single umbrella.

In the last couple of years, C.V. Rajan has been actively writing in both English and Tamil at the popular website quora.com.

Contact the Author

Dear Reader,

Did you read the book and find it useful for you? Did you find the book interesting? Do you have any feedback / review / suggestions/ criticism to offer? Kindly send a mail to me : rajan.chakra@gmail.com.

C. V. Rajan's other books

C. V. Rajan has been publishing his books predominantly as eBooks.

C. V. Rajan published his first Paperback titled 'How to Handle Anxiety and stress' from notionpress.com, which was, incidentally, his first eBook that was well received by readers.

You may please visit his Author's page at Amazon to have a look at his eBooks from this link --> *https://amazon.com/author/ cvrajan.sandeepika*

(See next page)

How Survive and Succeed in Office and Home Life

By C.V.Rajan

Understanding and Handling Anxiety and Stress

By C.V.Rajan

What is Love? Where is True Love?

By C.V.Rajan

புத்தம் புது கனவுகள்

By C.V.Rajan
சாந்தீபிகா

துணிவைத் தேடி

By C.V.Rajan
சாந்தீபிகா

Please visit: *https://amazon.com/author/cvrajan.sandeepika*

The above Paperback edition is available at
https://notionpress.com/read/understanding-and-handling-anxiety-and-stress